Interactive Computing Series

How to Create Web Pages Using HTML

Brief Edition

Kenneth C. Laudon • **Kenneth Rosenblatt**

David Langley

Boston   Burr Ridge, IL   Dubuque, IA   Madison, WI   New York   San Francisco   St. Louis
Bangkok   Bogotá   Caracas   Kuala Lumpur   Lisbon   London   Madrid   Mexico City
Milan   Montreal   New Delhi   Santiago   Seoul   Singapore   Sydney   Taipei   Toronto

McGraw-Hill Higher Education ✖

A Division of The **McGraw-Hill** Companies

HOW TO CREATE WEB PAGES USING HTML BRIEF EDITION
Published by McGraw-Hill/Irwin, an imprint of The McGraw-Hill
Companies, Inc., 1221 Avenue of the Americas, New York, NY 10020.

This book is printed on acid-free paper.

1 2 3 4 5 6 7 8 9 0 QPD/QPD 0 9 8 7 6 5 4 3 2 1

ISBN   0-07-247182-4

Publisher: *George Werthman*
Associate editor: *Steve Schuetz*
Developmental editor: *Diana Del Castillo*
Senior marketing manager: *Jeff Parr*
Senior project manager: *Pat Frederickson*
Senior production supervisor: *Michael R. McCormick*
Coordinator, freelance design: *Pam Verros*
Supplement producer: *Mark Mattson*
Senior producer, media technology: *David Barrick*
Cover design: *JoAnne Schopler*
Interior designer: *Asylum Studios*
Cover photograph: *Bill Brooks/© Masterfile*
Compositor: *Azimuth Interactive, Inc.*
Typeface: *10/12 Times*
Printer: *Quebecor Printing Book Group/Dubuque*

Library of Congress Control Number: 2001099185

www.mhhe.com

InformationTechnology

Information Technology at McGraw-Hill/Irwin

At McGraw-Hill Higher Education, we publish instructional materials targeted at the higher education market. In an effort to expand the tools of higher learning, we publish texts, lab manuals, study guides, testing materials, software, and multimedia products.

At McGraw-Hill/Irwin (a division of McGraw-Hill Higher Education), we realize that technology has created and will continue to create new mediums for professors and students to use in managing resources and communicating information with one another. We strive to provide the most flexible and complete teaching and learning tools available as well as offer solutions to the changing world of teaching and learning.

MCGRAW-HILL/IRWIN IS DEDICATED TO PROVIDING THE TOOLS FOR TODAY'S INSTRUCTORS AND STUDENTS TO SUCCESSFULLY NAVIGATE THE WORLD OF INFORMATION TECHNOLOGY.

- **Seminar series**—Technology Connection seminar series offered across the country every year demonstrates the latest technology products and encourages collaboration among teaching professionals.

- **Osborne/McGraw-Hill**—This division of The McGraw-Hill Companies is known for its best-selling Internet titles: Harley Hahn's Internet & Web Yellow Pages, and the Internet Complete Reference. Osborne offers an additional resource for certification and has strategic publishing relationships with corporations such as Corel Corporation and America Online. For more information visit Osborne at www.osborne.com.

- **Digital solutions**—McGraw-Hill/Irwin is committed to publishing digital solutions. Taking your course online does not have to be a solitary venture, nor does it have to be a difficult one. We offer several solutions that will allow you to enjoy all the benefits of having course material online. For more information visit www.mhhe.com/solutions/index.mhtml.

- **Packaging options**—For more about our discount options, contact your local McGraw-Hill/Irwin Sales representative at 1-800-338-3987 or visit our Web site at www.mhhe.com/it.

Interactive Computing Series

GOALS/PHILOSOPHY

The *Interactive Computing Series* provides you with an illustrated interactive environment for learning software skills using Microsoft Office. The text uses both "hands-on" instruction, supplementary text, and independent exercises to enrich the learning experience.

APPROACH

The *Interactive Computing Series* is the visual interactive way to develop and apply software skills. This skills-based approach coupled with its highly visual, two-page spread design allows the student to focus on a single skill without having to turn the page. A Lesson Goal at the beginning of each lesson prepares the student to apply the skills with a real-world focus. The Quiz and Interactivity sections at the end of each lesson measure the student's understanding of the concepts and skills learned in the two-page spreads and reinforce the skills with additional exercises.

ABOUT THE BOOK

The **Interactive Computing Series** offers *two levels* of instruction. Each level builds upon the previous level.

Brief lab manual—covers the basics of the application, contains two to four chapters.

Introductory lab manual—includes the material in the Brief textbook plus two to four additional chapters. The Introductory lab manuals prepare students for the *Microsoft Office User Specialist Proficiency Exam (MOUS Certification)*.

Each lesson is divided into a number of Skills. Each **Skill** is first explained at the top of the page in the Concept. Each **Concept** is a concise description of why the Skill is useful and where it is commonly used. Each **Step (Do It!)** contains the instructions on how to complete the Skill. The appearance of the ***MOUS Skill*** icon on a Skill page indicates that the Skill contains instruction in at least one of the required MOUS objectives for the relevant exam. Though the icons appear in the Brief manuals as well as the Introductory manuals, only the Introductory manuals may be used in preparation for MOUS Certification.

Figure 1

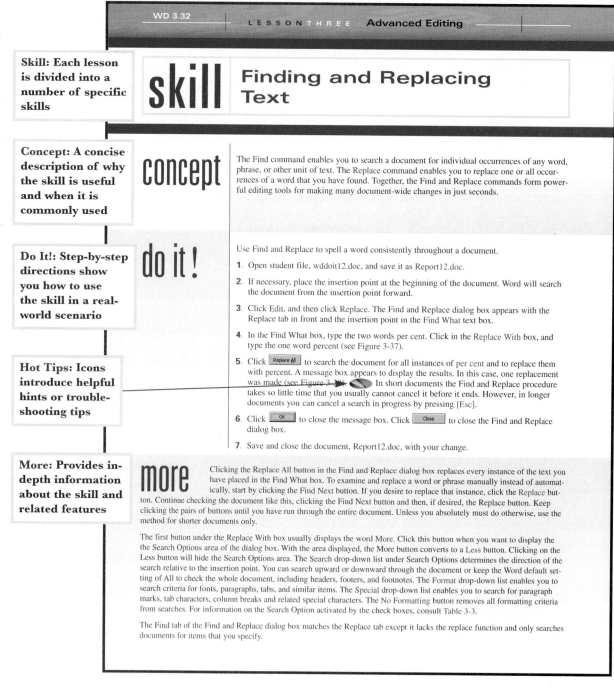

Skill: Each lesson is divided into a number of specific skills

Concept: A concise description of why the skill is useful and when it is commonly used

Do It!: Step-by-step directions show you how to use the skill in a real-world scenario

Hot Tips: Icons introduce helpful hints or trouble-shooting tips

More: Provides in-depth information about the skill and related features

---

WD 3.32   LESSON THREE   Advanced Editing

skill   Finding and Replacing Text

concept

The Find command enables you to search a document for individual occurrences of any word, phrase, or other unit of text. The Replace command enables you to replace one or all occurrences of a word that you have found. Together, the Find and Replace commands form powerful editing tools for making many document-wide changes in just seconds.

do it!

Use Find and Replace to spell a word consistently throughout a document.

1. Open student file, wddoit12.doc, and save it as Report12.doc.

2. If necessary, place the insertion point at the beginning of the document. Word will search the document from the insertion point forward.

3. Click Edit, and then click Replace. The Find and Replace dialog box appears with the Replace tab in front and the insertion point in the Find What text box.

4. In the Find What box, type the two words per cent. Click in the Replace With box, and type the one word percent (see Figure 3-37).

5. Click Replace All to search the document for all instances of per cent and to replace them with percent. A message box appears to display the results. In this case, one replacement was made (see Figure 3-38). In short documents the Find and Replace procedure takes so little time that you usually cannot cancel it before it ends. However, in longer documents you can cancel a search in progress by pressing [Esc].

6. Click OK to close the message box. Click Close to close the Find and Replace dialog box.

7. Save and close the document, Report12.doc, with your change.

more

Clicking the Replace All button in the Find and Replace dialog box replaces every instance of the text you have placed in the Find What box. To examine and replace a word or phrase manually instead of automatically, start by clicking the Find Next button. If you desire to replace that instance, click the Replace button. Continue checking the document like this, clicking the Find Next button and then, if desired, the Replace button. Keep clicking the pairs of buttons until you have run through the entire document. Unless you absolutely must do otherwise, use the method for shorter documents only.

The first button under the Replace With box usually displays the word More. Click this button when you want to display the the Search Options area of the dialog box. With the area displayed, the More button converts to a Less button. Clicking on the Less button will hide the Search Options area. The Search drop-down list under Search Options determines the direction of the search relative to the insertion point. You can search upward or downward through the document or keep the Word default setting of All to check the whole document, including headers, footers, and footnotes. The Format drop-down list enables you to search criteria for fonts, paragraphs, tabs, and similar items. The Special drop-down list enables you to search for paragraph marks, tab characters, column breaks and related special characters. The No Formatting button removes all formatting criteria from searches. For information on the Search Option activated by the check boxes, consult Table 3-3.

The Find tab of the Find and Replace dialog box matches the Replace tab except it lacks the replace function and only searches documents for items that you specify.

In the book, each skill is described in a two-page graphical spread (Figure 1). The left side of the two-page spread describes the skill, the concept, and the steps needed to perform the skill. The right side of the spread uses screen shots to show you how the screen should look at key stages.

Figure 1 (cont'd)

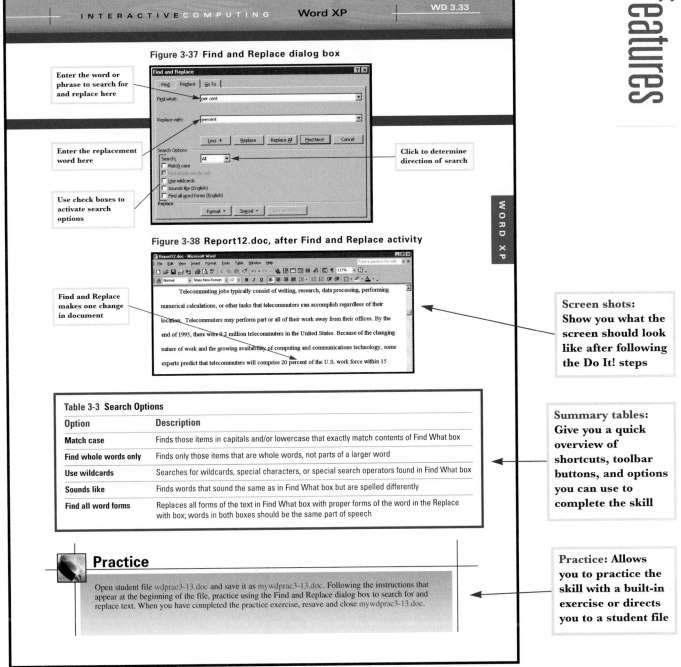

INTERACTIVE COMPUTING **Word XP** WD 3.33

WORD XP

Figure 3-37 Find and Replace dialog box

Enter the word or phrase to search for and replace here

Enter the replacement word here

Use check boxes to activate search options

Click to determine direction of search

Figure 3-38 Report12.doc, after Find and Replace activity

Find and Replace makes one change in document

Screen shots: Show you what the screen should look like after following the Do It! steps

Telecommuting jobs typically consist of writing, research, data processing, performing numerical calculations, or other tasks that telecommuters can accomplish regardless of their location. Telecommuters may perform part or all of their work away from their offices. By the end of 1995, there were 9.2 million telecommuters in the United States. Because of the changing nature of work and the growing availability of computing and communications technology, some experts predict that telecommuters will comprise 20 percent of the U.S. work force within 15

Table 3-3 Search Options

Option	Description
Match case	Finds those items in capitals and/or lowercase that exactly match contents of Find What box
Find whole words only	Finds only those items that are whole words, not parts of a larger word
Use wildcards	Searches for wildcards, special characters, or special search operators found in Find What box
Sounds like	Finds words that sound the same as in Find What box but are spelled differently
Find all word forms	Replaces all forms of the text in Find What box with proper forms of the word in the Replace with box; words in both boxes should be the same part of speech

Summary tables: Give you a quick overview of shortcuts, toolbar buttons, and options you can use to complete the skill

Practice

Open student file wdprac3-13.doc and save it as mywdprac3-13.doc. Following the instructions that appear at the beginning of the file, practice using the Find and Replace dialog box to search for and replace text. When you have completed the practice exercise, resave and close mywdprac3-13.doc.

Practice: Allows you to practice the skill with a built-in exercise or directs you to a student file

END-OF-LESSON FEATURES

In the book, the learning in each lesson is reinforced at the end by a Quiz and a skills review called Interactivity, which provides step-by-step exercises and real-world problems for the students to solve independently.

The following is a list of supplemental material available with the Interactive Computing Series:

Skills Assessment

SimNet eXPert (Simulated Network Assessment Product)—SimNet provides a way for you to test students' software skills in a simulated environment. SimNet is available for Microsoft Office 97, Microsoft Office 2000, and Microsoft Office XP. SimNet provides flexibility for you in your course by offering:

• Pre-testing options
• Post-testing options
• Course placement testing
• Diagnostic capabilities to reinforce skills
• Proficiency testing to measure skills
• Web or LAN delivery of tests
• Computer based training materials (New for Office XP)
• MOUS preparation exams
• Learning verification reports
• Spanish Version

Instructor's Resource Kits

The Instructor's Resource Kit provides professors with all of the ancillary material needed to teach a course. McGraw-Hill/Irwin is dedicated to providing instructors with the most effective instruction resources available. Many of these resources are available at our Information Technology Supersite www.mhhe.com/it. Our Instructor's Kits are available on CD-ROM and contain the following:

Diploma by Brownstone—is the most flexible, powerful, and easy-to-use computerized testing system available in higher education. The diploma system allows professors to create an Exam as a printed version, as a LAN-based Online version, and as an Internet version. Diploma includes grade book features, which automate the entire testing process.

Instructor's Manual—Includes:
–Solutions to all lessons and end-of-unit material
–Teaching Tips
–Teaching Strategies
–Additional exercises

PowerPoint Slides—NEW to the *Interactive Computing Series*, all of the figures from the application textbooks are available in PowerPoint slides for presentation purposes.

Student Data Files—To use the *Interactive Computing Series*, students must have Student Data Files to complete practice and test sessions. The instructor and students using this text in classes are granted the right to post the student files on any network or stand-alone computer, or to distribute the files on individual diskettes. The student files may be downloaded from our IT Supersite at www.mhhe.com/it.

Series Web Site—Available at www.mhhe.com/cit/apps/laudon.

Digital Solutions

Pageout—is our Course Web site Development Center. Pageout offers a Syllabus page, Web site address, Online Learning Center Content, online exercises and quizzes, gradebook, discussion board, an area for students to build their own Web pages, and all the features of Pageout Lite. For more information please visit the Pageout Web site at www.mhla.net/pageout.

Digital Solutions (continued)

OLC/Series Web Sites—Online Learning Centers (OLCs)/Series Sites are accessible through our Supersite at www.mhhe.com/it. Our Online Learning Centers/Series Sites provide pedagogical features and supplements for our titles online. Students can point and click their way to key terms, learning objectives, chapter overviews, PowerPoint slides, exercises, and Web links.

The McGraw-Hill Learning Architecture (MHLA)—is a complete course delivery system. MHLA gives professors ownership in the way digital content is presented to the class through online quizzing, student collaboration, course administration, and content management. For a walk-through of MHLA visit the MHLA Web site at www.mhla.net.

Packaging Options—For more about our discount options, contact your local McGraw-Hill/Irwin Sales representative at 1-800-338-3987 or visit our Web site at www.mhhe.com/it.

Visit www.mhhe.com/it
THE ONLY SITE WITH ALL YOUR CIT AND MIS NEEDS.

acknowledgments

The *Interactive Computing Series* is a cooperative effort of many individuals, each contributing to an overall team effort. The Interactive Computing team is composed of instructional designers, writers, multimedia designers, graphic artists, and programmers. Our goal is to provide you and your instructor with the most powerful and enjoyable learning environment using both traditional text and interactive techniques. Interactive Computing is tested rigorously prior to publication.

Our special thanks to George Werthman, our Publisher; Diana Del Castillo, our Developmental Editor; and Jeffrey Parr, Marketing Director for Computer Information Systems. They have provided exceptional market awareness and understanding, along with enthusiasm and support for the project, and have inspired us all to work closely together. In addition, Steven Schuetz provided valuable technical review of our interactive versions, and Charles Pelto contributed superb quality assurance.

The Azimuth team members who contributed to the *Interactive Computing Series* are:

Ken Rosenblatt (Editorial Director, Writer)
Russell Polo (Technical Director)
Robin Pickering (Developmental Editor, Writer)
David Langley (Writer)

Interactive Computing Series

How to Create Web Pages Using HTML

Brief Edition

Contents

How to Create Web Pages
Using HTML Brief Edition

Using HTML continued

Introduction to Web Pages

Designing Web pages is a creative adventure. You will need to use your creative instincts for color, text, images, and style in order to create useful and attractive Web pages. You will also need a good sense of organization because useful Web pages are well-organized collections of information.

HTML (Hypertext Markup Language) is a programming language used to create Web pages. You can use an ordinary word processor to create HTML documents that all Web browsers can understand and interpret. HTML may at first appear difficult to understand, but in fact it is a very simple language that you can learn in a few hours. The most difficult part of building useful Web pages is not learning HTML, but selecting the colors, text, images and other elements of Web pages.

Many people use graphical HTML editors such as Microsoft FrontPage, Adobe PageMill, or Macromedia Dreamweaver to create Web pages without learning HTML. These graphical editors generate HTML code automatically based on your commands and instructions. However, it is quite often necessary to edit the HTML produced by these programs. Also, you will be limited by the features provided by the programs. By learning HTML you will be able to edit and enhance the Web pages produced by these graphical programs.

Lesson Goal:

In this lesson, you will learn how to plan and organize a Web site; how to create HTML documents and Web pages; how to enter text and add graphics onto your Web pages, and how to create hyperlinks to other Web sites. Once you have mastered the basics, you will learn more advanced skills like creating forms and publishing Web pages.

skills

≶ **Introducing HTML**

≶ **Introduction to Web Browsers**

≶ **Using a Text Editor**

≶ **Opening a Document to View its HTML Structure**

≶ **Understanding Tags**

≶ **Writing Tags and Editing HTML Pages**

≶ **Saving Pages**

≶ **Printing an HTML Document**

≶ **Planning a Web Site**

skill

Introducing HTML

concept

HTML, or Hypertext Markup Language, is a programming language used to create Web pages. Don't let the name scare you. While you will need to learn some simple commands, you don't need to become a computer programmer. All it takes to learn basic HTML is a few hours of reading and practicing.

HTML instructions, called tags, tell the Web browser what to display and how to display it. HTML tags describe the content of a document in detail. For example, tags tell the browser how to format text, what background color to use, and whether to display an image or a hyperlink.

HTML documents are plain text or ASCII files that are translated by programs called Web browsers to display the resulting Web page. They look like text scattered with less than and greater than symbols (< and >) until you open them in a browser. HTML enables you to add rules, graphics, sound, and even video. HTML documents are saved in a text-only format that all computers can read and interpret.

HTML is an evolving language. In 1994 the World Wide Web Consortium (W3C) was founded to develop common standards for its development. However, in practice, competition between the two major browser manufacturers, Microsoft and Netscape Communications, compromise the universality of HTML. Each company creates new extensions to try to woo the Web surfing public to their product. Understanding how HTML works will enable you to stay abreast of the latest innovations. This knowledge will also help you decide what special effects to use based on how universal you want your page to be and who your intended audience is.

Many people never notice the HTML source page. When you surf the Internet you are viewing your Web browser's interpretation of an HTML source document. To view the source document, choose either View HTML Source or View Source from your browser's View menu. In fact, this is one of the best ways to become familiar with HTML design principles. You can even download the source document, save it to your hard drive, reopen it in a basic text editor, enter your own content, and open the file in your Web browser to learn what the Web authors did and how they did it. Copyright considerations cannot be ignored however, so use others' pages for inspiration and as a learning device only.

In this book you will learn how to structure and write the commands or tags, used in HTML and how to use them to create Web pages to your specifications.

Figure 1-1 displays the HTML source for the National Oceanic and Atmospheric Association's (NOAA) home page on the Internet. While it may look confusing to you now, it will not take long for you to learn which HTML commands are related to which graphical elements. If you look carefully, you will notice that HTML is written in English, but uses abbreviations that are easy to learn and use.

Figure 1-2 is the same Web page shown in Figure 1-1, viewed through a Web browser. The HTML shown in Figure 1-1 tells the browser to display the page seen in Figure 1-2.

Figure 1-1 HTML source of NOAA home page

Tags

HTML Code

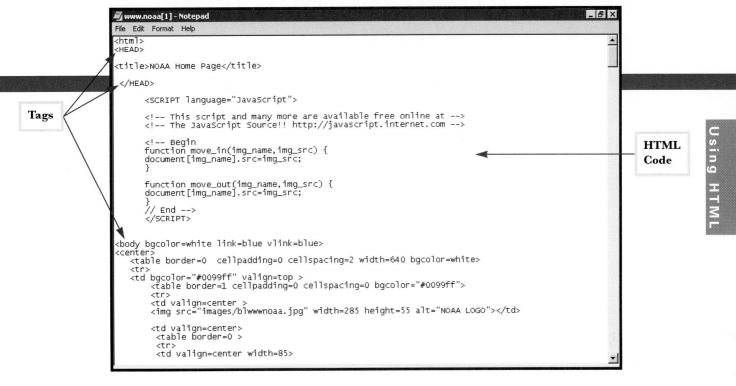

Figure 1-2 NOAA home page, as displayed by a Web browser

Graphic

Formatted text

Hyperlink

skill | Introduction to Web Browsers

concept

A Web browser is a computer program that interprets the commands found in HTML documents and converts those commands into a properly formatted Web page that appears on your screen. A very powerful feature of HTML and Web browser programs is that they are multi-platform. For instance, an HTML document on a Windows personal computer will appear nearly identical when displayed on a Macintosh personal computer or a Unix workstation. This means that no matter what type of personal computer you have, or where in the world you are located, you can use the Web. That's why it is called "The World Wide Web."

There are, however, slight differences among major brands of browsers. The two market-leading browsers are Microsoft's Internet Explorer and Netscape's Navigator browser. Each company has given their browser programs proprietary extensions or capabilities not shared by the other. This produces slight differences in the Web page display. Therefore, when you are designing Web pages you should have a copy of both major browsers to test your pages and ensure they display properly.

It is also wise to consider that not everyone in the world will have a high-speed modem connection or a fast computer. In fact, much of the world is still using older 486 computers with older operating systems that have difficulty displaying graphics. When designing your Web pages you may want to keep them simple and rely more on text in order to achieve the largest possible audience.

Figure 1-3 shows you the NOAA page again, viewed in the Netscape Navigator browser. Figure 1-4 shows the same page viewed through the Internet Explorer browser. The HTML source document for the page is the same, but different browsers may interpret it differently.

In the case of the NOAA home page, the page looks almost the same in both browsers because the page was specifically designed to work with both Netscape Navigator and Internet Explorer. Another browser may not be able to display some of the fonts or images, or some of the other elements that are included in the page.

Figure 1-3 NOAA home page viewed in Netscape Navigator

Figure 1-4 NOAA home page viewed in Microsoft Internet Explorer

skill | Using a Text Editor

concept

You can create an HTML document using any text editor. A text editor is a simple word processing program. Using these free tools that come with your operating system, you can write HTML and save it in ASCII or plain text format to produce Web pages. For the exercises in this book, we will use the text editor, Notepad, which comes with Microsoft Windows. Other text editors you can use to write HTML are Wordpad for Windows, Pico for Unix, or Teach Text for Mac.

do it !

Open the text editor Notepad from Microsoft Windows.

1. Click ⊞Start on the Windows taskbar. The Start menu appears.

2. Select Programs from the menu. The Programs submenu appears.

3. Place the mouse pointer over Accessories. The Accessories submenu appears.

4. Place the mouse pointer over Notepad, as shown in Figure 1-5. (Because the Windows Desktop is customizable, yours may not look exactly like the one shown in Figure 1-5.) Click the left mouse button.

5. The Notepad program opens, as shown in Figure 1-6.

more

Click the left mouse button once unless otherwise indicated. You may also be instructed to right-click (click the right mouse button once) or double-click (click the left mouse button twice in rapid succession).

Notepad opens to a blank document. You will see a flashing black line called the insertion point. The insertion point tells you where the text will appear when you begin typing. You can place the insertion point (and thus the place where text will appear) by pressing the [Spacebar] or the [Enter] key.

Figure 1-5 Windows Desktop

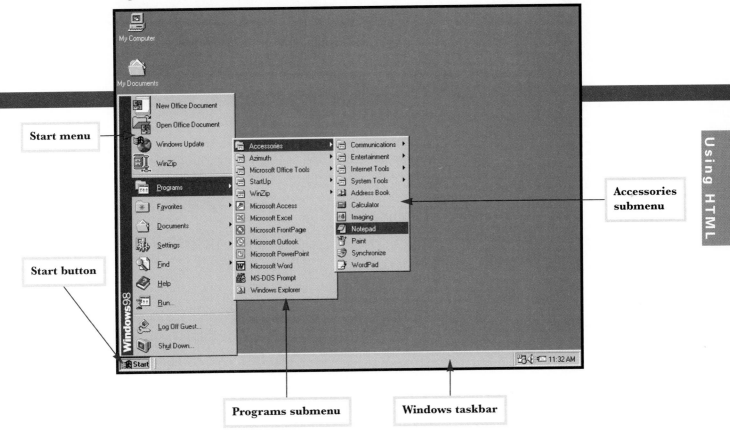

Start menu

Start button

Accessories submenu

Programs submenu

Windows taskbar

Figure 1-6 Notepad Application/Window

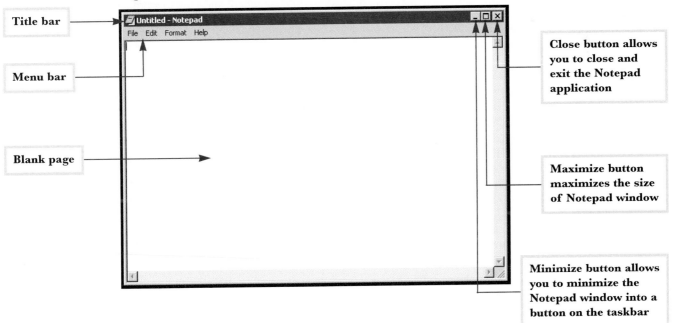

Title bar

Menu bar

Blank page

Close button allows you to close and exit the Notepad application

Maximize button maximizes the size of Notepad window

Minimize button allows you to minimize the Notepad window into a button on the taskbar

skill | Opening a Document to View its HTML Structure

concept

All HTML pages adhere to a basic structure. You should learn this basic structure before you try to write HTML tags or commands. You must also know how to open a document written in a text editor, so that you can open HTML documents that you are working on.

do it !

Open an HTML document in Notepad and view the basic HTML page structure that every Web page includes.

1. Click File on the Menu bar. The File menu opens.

2. Click Open on the File menu. The Open dialog box opens.

3. Click the list arrow in the Look in list box to locate the Student Files folder, as shown in Figure 1-7. Once you have located it, double-click it. The contents of the folder will be displayed, which are four additional folders, named Lesson 1, Lesson 2, and so on.

4. Since you currently are working in Lesson 1 of this book, double-click the Lesson 1 folder to open it. Then click the file htdoit1-4.txt to select it. Click [Open]. The file is opened in Notepad, as shown in Figure 1-8. This figure shows the basic structure of an HTML page. Steps 3 and 4 assume that you or your instructor have previously stored the Student Files associated with this text on the Windows desktop. However, to protect your work and that of other students from accidental or deliberate damage and loss, your instructor may give you other directions on where and how to store and open your files.

5. Close the file, which will also close the Notepad application.

more

Every HTML page starts and ends with HTML tags. These tags indicate to the browser that an HTML source document will follow. The Head tag tells the browser that what immediately follows is the heading section of the document. The page's heading or title will appear in the browser's Title bar, and thus in any bookmarks or favorites folders and in search engine listings. You can also place messages and headers in this area. The first Body tag designates the beginning of the actual content. All text and page elements will be enclosed in the Body tags. You are now ready to begin creating Web pages with HTML. Once you learn more commands you can simply plug them into this template.

Unlike sophisticated word processing programs that will remain active if you close only a file within them, the Notepad application automatically closes when you close a Notepad file. Notepad also will not keep a previously opened file active if you open an additional file. Instead, the additional file will open, and the previously opened one will close. Similarly, if you click the File menu, then click the New command, a blank file will open, and any previously opened one will close. To keep Notepad running while working on multiple files, therefore, you must open one file after another (always remembering that each new file will close the previous one). To return to and work on a previously saved file, simply click the File menu, click the Open command, and then select and open the desired file.

Figure 1-7 Open dialog box

List box

List menu

Automatically views the files and folders on your desktop

Allows you to view a previous folder in the folder hierarchy

Place the pointer over Student Files to select Student Files folder

List arrow

Figure 1-8 Basic structure of an HTML page in Notepad

HTML page structure

Practice

Open htprac1-4.txt in Notepad. Carefully review the three major parts of the HTML page structure and close the file.

skill ‧ Understanding Tags

concept

Tags are commands in HTML that are written between angle brackets: < >. Tags instruct a browser to display page elements in a certain way. Most tags require an opening tag and a closing tag to execute the command properly. An opening tag is written as <TAG>. A closing tag is written as </TAG>. The closing tag contains a forward slash, /. Text contained outside the opening and closing tags will not be affected by the commands. Tags should be written in capital letters, if for no other reason than to differentiate them from the rest of the text. You can write tags in capital letters by holding the [Shift] key while pressing letter keys, or by pressing the [Caps Lock] key, and typing normally. Although typing your tags in capital letters makes them easier to find in source pages, the source codes of many Web sites—including ones referenced in this book—contain lower-case tags. Tags in lowercase will function just like ones in capital letters.

Figure 1-9 displays the basic HTML page structure we viewed earlier. Notice the opening tag, <HTML>. This tag indicates that what follows will be in HTML. The final line, </HTML>, designates the end of the page.

Text on a page may be affected by more than one set of tags. For example, the opening body tag, <BODY>, and closing body tag, </BODY> are contained within the HTML tags. Therefore all text contained within the Body tags is affected by both the body commands and the HTML commands. When we begin to add more specific commands, the text will be affected by all tags in which it is enclosed. Figure 1-10, the HTML source for the National Aeronautics and Space Administration (NASA) home page, illustrates the use of multiple tags. As a rule, all tags that appear within another set of tags should close within that set, as follows: <A><B>text</B></A>.

Tags may also include commands called attributes. Attributes affect specific features of a page such as background color, font, or the size of an object. Tags with attributes are written like this: <TAG ATTRIBUTE>. You can add as many attributes as you desire. The use of attributes is also illustrated in Figure 1-10.

Finally, when you write tags with attributes, you will have to specify values. Values indicate how an attribute should appear. For example, when you create a table you will have to specify the border thickness of the table and the color of text. A value can be a number, color, or any other type of information. Values are generally enclosed in quotation marks, as follows: <TAG ATTRIBUTE="VALUE">. Figure 1-10 also illustrates the use of values.

HTML browsers do not automatically add the spaces you insert in the source document into your Web page. Adding spaces and returns while you design and edit your HTML source document helps to maintain clarity, but do not use them to format the Web page. For example, if we added text between the Head and Body tags in Figure 1-9, the sentences would not appear on separate lines on the Web page. Instead, they would appear consecutively. Commands must be added to create paragraphs, spaces, and line breaks. Certain tags automatically create new lines or spaces on a Web page. For example, the Header tag automatically includes a line break, and the List Item tag automatically creates a new line for each line of text.

Figure 1-9 Basic HTML page structure

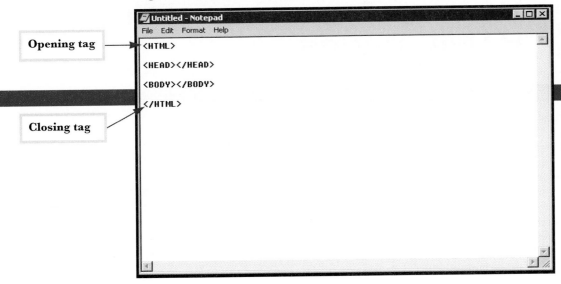

Opening tag

Closing tag

Figure 1-10 HTML source for NASA home page

Body tag marks the opening of the body of the page

Attribute for specifying background color for entire page

Tag

Attribute

Value

Value for the actual color that is specified by the attribute

Practice

View a Web page in your browser. Then view the HTML source of the page. This can be done by selecting HTML Source, Page Source, or View Source from your browser's View Menu. Identify the tags, values, and attributes in the HTML source. Close the browser and the HTML source of the page.

skill | Writing Tags and Editing HTML Pages

concept

Now that you are familiar with the overview behind tags, attributes and values, it is time for you to begin writing basic tags. It will take time and patience at first while you learn the common symbols, such as the forward slash and the angle brackets, which comprise HTML code. After you learn these basic tags, you will be ready to work with more complex tags.

do it !

Create a Web page in HTML. You will start by creating some of the basic tags that every Web page requires.

1. Open the Notepad program. It should open to a blank page with a blinking insertion point in the top-left corner of the workspace.

2. Hold the [Shift] key and press the [,] key at the same time.

3. Type: HTML. Then hold the [Shift] key again and press the [.] at the same time.

4. Press the [Enter] key twice.

5. Using the same method as above, type <BODY>. Press the [Enter] key again.

6. Type </BODY>. Press the [Enter] key twice.

7. Type: </HTML>. Your page should now look like Figure 1-11. When you have a problem with an element not appearing correctly on your page, it is usually caused by a tag error. Sometimes a closing tag is omitted, or it does not have a backslash to identify it as a closing tag.

8. Notice that if you place the pointer around on the page it will turn into an I-beam. Place the I-beam at the beginning of the blank line in between the opening HTML tag and the opening Body tag and click. The insertion point is now where you clicked the I-beam. Press the [Enter] key.

9. Type: <HEAD>, and press the [Enter] key.

10. Type: </HEAD>, and press the [Enter] key. Your page should now look like Figure 1-12.

11. Close the file without saving it.

more

Even though browsers do not recognize them, it is advisable to add plenty of spaces to your HTML source document, especially the first few times you design a Web page. This will keep you from confusing different tags or improperly writing tags so that a browser will be unable to read them. The extra spaces will not affect the appearance of the Web page, but will keep your work clear and understandable.

To edit your HTML document, place the insertion point behind (i.e., just to the left of) the text that you want to delete. Then press the [Delete] key until you have removed all of the desired characters and spaces. Alternately, you can place the insertion point after (just to the right of) the text, then press the [Backspace] key until you have removed all desired characters and spaces. You can also double-click on the text to select it, then press the [Delete], [Backspace], or [Enter] key to delete the text, or simply begin typing to replace it.

Figure 1-11 Basic HTML tags

Opening Tags

Closing tags

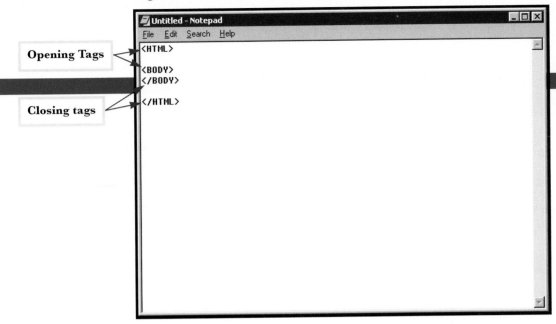

Figure 1-12 Basic HTML page structure

Head tags
mark the
Head section
of the page

Practice

Open Notepad and create an HTML page structure identical to the one in Figure 1-12. Save and close the file as htprac1-6.txt.

skill | Saving Pages

concept

A crucial part of working with any computer-generated document, including HTML source documents, is to save your work. Although a simple Web page can be written in a few hours, more complex pages will take considerably longer to design. You will need to know how to save your document and how to select the correct format in which to save it. Periodically saving your work while you are composing is always prudent to prevent data loss in the event of a power outage or computer failure.

do it !

Save an HTML source document with a different name.

1. Open Notepad.

2. Open the file htdoit1-7.txt.

3. Click File on the Menu bar.

4. Click Save As. The Save As dialog box opens.

5. Choose Desktop in the Save in list box. ◕ As noted in a previous skill, your instructor may give you other directions on where and how to store your files.

6. Double-click in the File name: text box. Type: home. As the desktop is customizable, your dialog box may not look exactly the same as Figure 1-13.

7. Click Save . Notice that the Title bar has changed to reflect the new name, as shown in Figure 1-14.

more

The Notepad document home now appears on your desktop with an icon. You can open the document by going through the process we described earlier, or you can simply double-click on the icon representing the document you want to open.

The Save command and the Save As command perform different functions. The first time you save a document, either command will open the Save As dialog box. However, after you have named a file and saved it in a specific location, the Save command will simply overwrite the existing document. The Save As command will enable you to change the name and/or location of the document. It allows you to make changes to and save a document with a new name while maintaining the original file under the initial file name. Both commands are accessed from the File menu.

To create a Web page from an HTML source document, type .html after the name of the page in the File name text box. For example, in the exercise above, you would have typed home.html. This will save the document as a Web page. ◕ Most home pages are titled either home.html, or index.html. Once you have saved a document as a Web page, it will open in your browser no matter where you have saved it. The document will also have a Web page icon rather than a Notepad icon.

Figure 1-13 Save As dialog box

Allows you to create a new folder in which to save the document

Allows you to select the format in which a document is saved

Figure 1-14 HTML document after it has been saved

Title bar contains the name of the document

Practice

Open file htprac1-7.txt in Notepad. Save it on your desktop as Index.html and close the file.

skill Printing an HTML Document

concept

You may want to create a hard copy of the HTML document on which you are working. It is often easier to revise a printed document. You can make notes in the margins and correct tag errors that you may have missed on the screen. To do this, you must be able to print an HTML source document.

do it !

Print an HTML document.

1. Open the index2.txt file in Notepad. Click File on the Menu bar (see Figure 1-15).

2. Click Page Setup. The Page Setup dialog box opens. Make sure your Page Setup dialog box looks like Figure 1-16. If necessary, make changes in the dialog box options so its settings resemble those in Figure 1-16.

3. Click ⎡ Printer... ⎤. Page Setup dialog box opens, as shown in Figure 1-17. Make sure the correct printer is selected. ◕ Clicking ⎡ Printer... ⎤, then clicking ⎡ Properties... ⎤ in the Page Setup dialog box allows you to select options, two-sided printing, increased color intensity and various font capabilities.

4. Click ⎡ OK ⎤. Then, click ⎡ OK ⎤ again.

5. Click File on the Menu bar. Then, click Print.

more

The Page Setup dialog box enables you to change how a document prints. For example, in the Size box of the Paper section, you can specify a default or custom paper size. In the Orientation section you can change the page orientation from vertical to horizontal by clicking the Landscape option button. In the Margins section, you can select the text in the Left, Right, Top, or Bottom boxes, then type new settings for your page margins.

Until now, you have worked mainly with Notepad files named htdoit1-4.txt, index2.txt, and so on. The .txt ending, or file extension, indicates plain text files. Such files are simple and thus easy to work with, even in other software programs. If you tried to open such files in a Web browser, they would open in Notepad instead. However, as explained earlier, saving a file in Notepad (or many other programs) with the .html file extension makes a file a Hypertext Markup Language file. You can open these types of files in any Web browser, and they will display the fonts, background colors, text locations, and so on that your HTML tags have specified. For example, an index2.htm file would display in a Web browser as shown in Figure 1-18.

Figure 1-15 Index2.txt file opened in Notepad

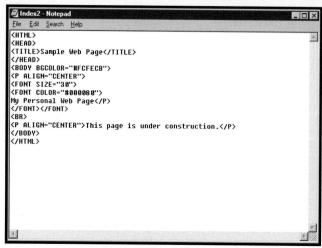

Figure 1-16 Page Setup dialog box

Specify the paper size

Preview of the printed page

Click to give horizontal orientation to page

Select boxes and type new settings to change page margins

Figure 1-17 Selecting a Printer

Name of the printer

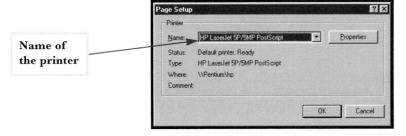

Figure 1-18 Index2.html file displayed in Web browser

Storage location of HTML file (your location may vary)

Practice

Print the Index.html page and close the file.

skill   Planning a Web Site

concept

Now that you are about to begin writing HTML documents and designing your own Web pages, you must take a step back and think carefully about the goals for your Web site. What do you want to accomplish?

Are you creating a business site or a personal forum for your own tastes and viewpoints? Planning your overall site organization, and the basic design and layout for individual pages, will save you time later. What information do you wish to convey? How many pages will you need, and what purpose will each page serve? Create an outline to answer these basic questions.

Consider how to hyperlink the pages within your site. (A hyperlink is a section of text or a graphic that, when clicked, takes Web site visitors to a destination page specified in the hyperlink.) After you have decided how to link your pages within your site, you can consider links to other sites. For example, if you are creating a NASA resource page, you might consider linking to NASA's home page or another page on the site that complements the information you are providing. Create a list of URLs you are interested in and determine the optimum placement for each link.

Somewhere along the line, especially as you add more pages, consider drawing a diagram of the overall Web site. Use boxes or rectangles to represent its individual pages and connecting lines to indicate the links between pages. As you revise the site, revise the diagram to help track which pages you have kept and how links have changed between pages. Ultimately, you want to have a site that is easy to navigate, no matter how many pages and links you have.

Decide what objects and features you want to include in your Web site. You may want to add graphics, or use tables to organize information. You may want to insert multimedia files, or create a background sound. You may want to use a simple background color, or create a background image. There are many elements you can add to Web pages, but you must decide for yourself which ones are right for your Web site. You should also consider your audience at this point. For example, does the site you have designed include lots of images, which often involve large file sizes that impede download time? Similarly, is your intended audience likely to have the necessary hardware to view video or play sounds?

One of the best ways to plan your own Web site is to view other people's work. Surf the Web to get an idea of the possibilities. Note the different styles, elements, and organizational structures that appeal to you and those that you find distasteful. Visit sites with similar topics to see how they present the subject matter. Make a list of the elements you want to include. Finally, devise a simple, consistent set of names for your pages, images and other external files. Distinctive page and file names are important for both the Web site author and the Web site visitor. The Web author will need them to ensure accurate link construction and the visitor will require them for accurate site navigation.

Figure 1-17 shows how colors, links, objects, and multimedia files can be used in a Web page.

Figure 1-19 National Weather Service home page

Links within Web site

Links to other related Web sites

Graphics and multi-media elements

shortcuts

Function	Opening Tag	Closing Tag
Signifies that the document is written in HTML	<HTML>	</HTML>
Signifies the beginning of the Web page	<HEAD>	</HEAD>
Signifies the body of the Web page	<BODY>	</BODY>
Tells the browser to display an attribute	<TAG ATTRIBUTE>	</TAG>
Tells the browser how to display that attribute	<TAG ATTRIBUTE="VALUE">	</TAG>

A. Identify Key Features

Name the items indicated by callouts in Figure 1-18.

Figure 1-20 An HTML source document

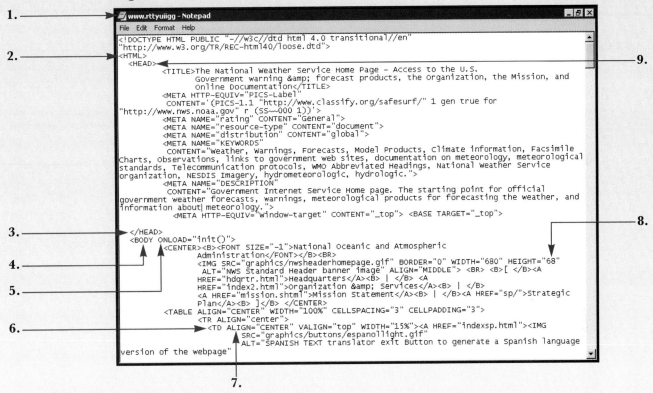

1.
2.
3.
4.
5.
6.
7.
8.
9.

B. Select the Best Answer

10. A programming language used to design Web Pages

11. A document that appears on the Internet with its own URL

12. A simple word processing program

13. Commands written in HTML

14. A program that allows you to view Web pages

15. All text and page elements are contained within this HTML document section

16. Affects specific features of a tag

17. Specifies the way attributes should appear

18. Command that allows you to change the way a page will look when it is printed

a. Attribute

b. Body

c. HTML

d. Page Setup

e. Tags

f. Text Editor

g. Value

h. Web browser

i. Web page

quiz (continued)

C. Complete the Statement

19. Most tags require the following in order to execute a command properly:

a. Message tags

b. Opening and closing tags

c. Capital letters

d. Different colors

20. If you want to view the HTML source of Web pages on the Internet:

a. You cannot because it is illegal

b. You must first obtain permission

c. You cannot because there is no way to view it

d. You will discover one of the best ways to learn HTML

21. All of the following are part of writing HTML except:

a. Linings

b. Tags

c. Attributes

d. Values

22. The best way to get ideas for your own Web site is to:

a. Poll as many people as possible

b. View as many similar Web sites as possible

c. Not let other Web sites influence you

d. Get someone to create it for you

23. If you forget to add a closing tag, or make another syntax error:

a. It will have no effect on your Web page

b. A good text editor will correct the problem

c. Your page will not display properly

d. A browser will still read the HTML source correctly

24. The Save As command allows you to:

a. Save the document under a new name and in a new location

b. Save the document under the same name and in the same location

c. Save the document under a new name but only in the same location

d. Save the document in a new location but under the same name

25. You can make a page print horizontally by:

a. Changing the paper size

b. Changing the margins

c. Changing the orientation to Portrait

d. Changing the orientation to Landscape

interactivity

Build Your Skills

1. Open a text editor:

   a. Click Start.

   b. Click Programs.

   c. Click Accessories.

   d. Click Notepad.

2. Open an HTML document:

   a. Click File. Click Open.

   b. Locate the Student Files folder.

   c. Open the Lesson 1 folder, then open the htskills1.txt document.

3. Write tags:

   a. Click File. Click New. Do not save changes to htskills1.txt.

   b. Type <HTML>. Press [Enter].

   c. Type <HEAD></HEAD>. Press [Enter].

   d. Type <BODY></BODY>. Press [Enter].

   e. Type </HTML>.

4. Save an HTML document:

   a. Click File. Click Save, which opens the Save As dialog box.

   b. In the Save in box, select the Desktop, or another storage destination desired by your instructor. Save the document as a text document with the file name Web Page.txt.

   c. Also save the document as a Web page with the file name Web Page.htm.

5. Print an HTML document:

   a. Click File. Click Page Setup.

   b. Make sure the correct printer is selected and is loaded with paper.

   c. Close the Page Setup dialog box.

   d. Click File. Click Print. Close the file, which will close Notepad.

interactivity (continued)

Problem Solving Exercises

1. Congratulations! You have been hired as a Webmaster at The Fixit Company. The Fixit Company sells hardware to construction companies, private consumers, and hardware stores all over the country. The executives at The Fixit Company have decided that they want a Web site in order to reach more potential customers and improve customer service. They have hired you to design a Web site for their company. Your first duty is to come up with some ideas to show your new boss. Start by visiting hardware sites on the Internet. Make notes on how many pages the typical hardware site has, how its pages are linked, what functions the pages fulfill, and what graphics and multimedia elements are included. Note what elements you like and dislike. Record your findings. Outline the basic structure and functions you think will be useful and potentially profitable for The Fixit Company to prepare for a meeting with the executives. When outlining the site, include (1) a product-ordering page, (2) a page where consumers can check order status, (3) a feedback/contact us page, and (4) a product list page complete with product descriptions. Remember that you do not have to create any actual pages here, just outline and describe the types of pages to create later.

2. Begin by creating the basic structure for the first Web page. First, open a text editor. You may use Word Pad, Notepad or any other text editor installed on your computer. Type the basic tags to construct a template that you can expand upon later. Start with the <HTML> tag and include Head and Body tags. Save this rudimentary file as Fixit.

3. You must also bring a copy of this basic structure to your bosses at The Fixit Company. First open the Fixit page, if it is not open already, and print two copies. Make sure there is plenty of spacing in your document. If not, create spacing so that the document will be easier to understand. Also make sure all of your tags are written correctly. For example, make sure that every tag has an opening and a closing tag. If they do not, the Web page will not display properly.

4. Plan another Web site, not for corporate purposes, but rather as your own personal forum. Base the site on your interests and make an outline of your plans. You may want to focus on a particular sport, musical group, or movie. Be creative and find a topic that really interests you. After you have decided on a topic, visit the Internet and search for similar sites. Again, note the elements you like and dislike, how many pages are in the site and how they are linked. You will use this plan to create your own Web site later on. Then create a template file with the basic structure of your Web site in your text editor, and save it as Personal.

Formatting Pages with HTML

In the previous lesson, you learned how to plan your Web site and create the basic structure for your Web pages. Now it's time to start building your Web pages by adding text, images, and links to other pages. What really makes a Web page interesting and unique is the way in which the Web author formats its text, and places objects, images, and other elements on the page.

There are now approximately 800 million Web pages in existence. Besides being an incomparable information resource, the Internet is a showcase that enables people to display information in entertaining, amusing, and artistic ways.

HTML offers Web authors the ability to include many sophisticated elements in their Web pages, such as titles, preformatted text, lists, tables, and hyperlinks. Generally, a hyperlink is an instruction that, when activated, links the user to a different Web page, either at the current site or another. However, you also can design hyperlinks that link from one area within a page to another area within the same page. The ability to link Web pages together and allow users to move quickly from one Web site to another is one of the most important features of HTML.

skills

* **Using Titles**

* **Adding and Formatting Text**

* **Working with Preformatted Text**

* **Using Paragraphs and Line Breaks**

* **Creating Lists**

* **Adding and Formatting Tables**

* **Understanding Anchors**

* **Creating Hyperlinks**

* **Adding Colors to a Web Page**

Lesson Goal:

In this lesson, you will learn how to add titles, format text, and work with pre-formatted text. Next, you will learn how to create paragraphs and insert line breaks. Then, you will learn how to add objects such as lists and tables and how to format them. Finally, you will learn how to add colors to a web page and create anchors and hyperlinks that allow users to move within HTML documents or to different Web sites.

skill Using Titles

concept

Every HTML page should have a title. The title appears in the browser's Title bar. Search engines, bookmarks and favorites lists also use the page's title, so it should provide an accurate page description and perhaps a keyword, to increase the likelihood that Web surfers searching for that topic will find your page. The Title tags are placed inside the Head tags.

do it !

Add a title to the home page.

1. Open the home document in Notepad.

2. Place the insertion point just to the right of the opening Head tag.

3. Press the [Enter] key.

4. Type: <TITLE>.

5. Type: Office Unbound—A New Direction in Management Training.

6. Type: </TITLE>.

7. Your document should look like Figure 2-1.

8. Click File on the Menu bar. Click Save to save the HTML source document.

9. Click File on the Menu bar. Click Save As. Save the document on your desktop as home.html. The icon for your page will look different, depending on what default browser you have.

10. If you double-click on the home icon, your page will look like Figure 2-2 in Internet Explorer. It will look similar in Netscape.

11. Close the browser.

more

Titles are also listed in a browser's history list. When you surf the Web, each page you visit is logged in the history list. If your page does not have a title, there will be a blank space on the history list where the title should be. Pages can be displayed without a title, but they may display improperly and will not receive the benefits of being listed in favorite or bookmark folders, history lists or search engines.

If you simply write your title inside the Head tags, and do not enclose it in the Title tags, it will appear as text at the top of your Web page.

Figure 2-1 Title in an HTML document

Title of a page is placed between opening and closing Title tags

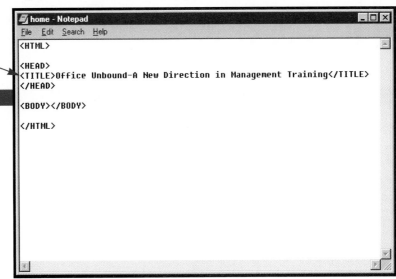

Figure 2-2 Title displayed in a Web browser

Title as it appears in a Web browser

Storage location of HTML page (your location may vary)

Practice

Add a title to a new HTML document. The title should be Don Knobley—Personal Accounting Firm. Save the file as title.html. If you have saved the file to the Desktop, double-click the icon located there to open and view the file in your Web browser, then close the file.

skill   Adding and Formatting Text

concept

Text is usually the single most important element on a Web page. It can be used for a variety of reasons beyond the obvious ones of conveying information and communicating ideas. Text can be used to emphasize a point, enliven a page with color, or to clarify a table or form with a caption. It can even be used as an alternative to images for visitors with browsers that do not support graphics or who have slow connections. You can customize text to complement the style of your Web site.

do it !

Add text to the home page, and format it using a Header tag and italics.

1. Place the insertion point after the closing Title tag. Press the [Enter] key.

2. Type: <H1>Office Unbound.</H1>.

3. Place the insertion point between the opening and closing Body tags. Press the [Enter] key.

4. Type: <I>A survival retreat, where your management personnel can get to know each other, enjoy a natural setting together, and most importantly, learn to work together, as a team.</I>. Press [Enter].

5. Your HTML document should look like Figure 2-3.

6. Click File on the Menu bar. Click Save As. Save the file as home.html. Click [Yes] to replace the existing file.

7. When you open the home page in a browser, it should look like Figure 2-4. ◖◗ If your Web page does look correct, double-check your Notepad file against the one in Figure 2-3, revise the file as needed, and resave it. To make the corrected version appears in your Web browser, click the browser's Refresh button (Internet Explorer) or the Reload button (Netscape Navigator).

8. Close the browser.

more

The <H> is a Header tag. It is an instruction to create a header in a certain pre-selected style. Instead of using specific tags to increase font size and make text bold, you can apply a Header tag. Headers are often used at the beginning of a page to construct a Table of Contents. There are six levels of Header tags. <H1> is the largest and most emphatic, and <H6> the smallest. It is not necessary to add attributes or values in order for browsers to interpret Header tags. However, remember that different browsers may display various modifications. So test your pages in several browsers to make sure you are satisfied with the results. ◖◗ To change the font size, use the following tag: <FONT SIZE="#">. The number should be between 1 and 7, 7 being the largest font size, 1 being the smallest. Add a + or — to make the font size relative to the base font, and thus even larger or smaller.

The <I> tag italicizes the enclosed text. Similar tags perform comparable functions. The Bold tag, <B>, for instance will make the enclosed text bold.

You can also use the tags <BIG> and <SMALL> to make text bigger or smaller relative to the surrounding text, without specifying an exact size value. Closing tags are required for all of the above tags.

Figure 2-3 Body text and a Header formatted in Notepad

Header tag that formats text in Header1

Body text contained within formatting tags

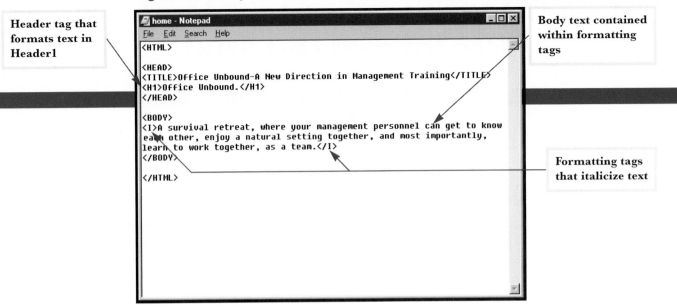

Formatting tags that italicize text

Figure 2-4 Home page as displayed in a browser

Header1 as viewed in a browser

Formatted, italicized body text

Practice

In the title.html file, create a Header, Don Knobley, in the Header 2 format. Then, in bold, write A Personal, Affordable, Accounting Firm within Body tags. Save the file and view it in a browser. Close the browser.

skill | Working with Preformatted Text

concept

It is often difficult to gauge exactly how your Web page will look on the Internet due to browser variables. Preformatted text enables you to display text in exactly the same layout as in your HTML source document. Your Web page retains the spacing and line breaks from the contained text in the HTML document. It is useful for designing simple tables and text graphics (ASCII art). The opening and closing tags for preformatted text are <PRE> and </PRE>. Preformatted text allows you to control the spacing and construct tables and lists without using the specific tags for lists and tables. Arrange the text in the desired format and enclose it in the <PRE> tags and all browsers will be able to read it.

do it !

Add preformatted text to your HTML document.

1. Open the home document in Notepad, if necessary. Place the insertion point after the closing Italics tag in the last paragraph you wrote.

2. Press [Enter] twice.

3. Type: <PRE>Call. Press [Enter].

4. Press [Tab]. Type the Underline tag, <U>, then type: 1-800-555-4563.

5. Type the closing Underline tag, </U>. Press [Enter].

6. Press [Tab]. Press [Tab] again. Type: to make an appointment today. </PRE>. Your document should look like Figure 2-5.

7. Click File on the Menu bar. Click Save.

8. Save the file as home.html.

9. If you open the Web page, it should look like Figure 2-6.

10. Close the browser.

more

You can also create space on your Web page without using preformatted text. Remember, normally when you add spaces and returns to your source document your browser does not recognize them. Only spacing that you add tags for will display. This is the major advantage of preformatted text. You can accurately space text on your source document and it will appear in exactly the same way in the browser.

You can add additional formatting to preformatted text, but it is advisable to wait until after you have viewed the document in your browser. Tags take up space in the source document but not the Web page. You will want to have the spacing correct on the Web page and then determine how to insert the extra tags so as not to disrupt the page layout.

Although we applied underlining to the phone number in the exercise, you should be careful about applying underlining because it is commonly used to designate a link. You may confuse visitors who expect underlined text to be a hyperlink.

Figure 2-5 Preformatted text in an HTML document

Preformatted Text opening tag →

Text contained within Preformatted Text tags

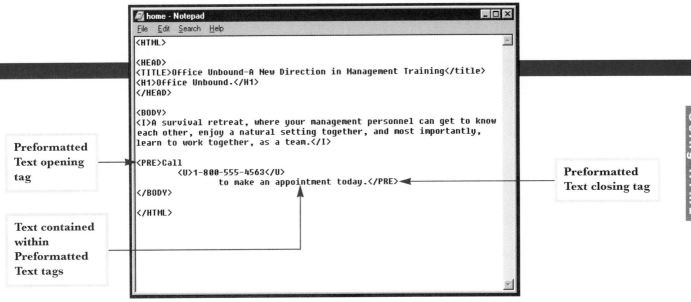

Preformatted Text closing tag

Figure 2-6 Preformatted text in a browser

Preformatted text appears exactly as it did in the HTML document

Practice

Create preformatted text in the title.html file. Press [Enter] after each phrase you type. Type: Low rates, Quick refunds, Knowledgeable staff, In-house tax attorney, and Experience. Save and close the file. Open and view the file in the Web browser of your choice.

skill | Using Paragraphs and Line Breaks

concept

Paragraphs can be created using the <P> tags, which break the text and insert a blank line. Line breaks can also be used to create space. The <BR> tags force a line break without inserting a blank line. Both tags start the text following the break on the left side of the page by default. The <BR> tag is useful for quotes or poems where you do not want the extra vertical space inserted. These two tags can help you to control the spacing of every element in your Web page.

do it !

Add a paragraph and a line break to the home page.

1. Open the home document in Notepad, if necessary. Place the insertion point behind the closing Preformatted Text tag.

2. Press [Enter] twice.

3. Type: <P>Our management crew was disorganized, and ineffective, but after the Office Unbound experience they're functioning as one big team.</P>.

4. Press [Enter].

5. Type:
Nancy Villones</BR>. Press [Enter].

6. Type: CEO of Marthop Enterprises. Your document should look like Figure 2-7.

7. Click File on the Menu bar. Click Save.

8. Save the document as home.html.

9. If you open the Web page in a browser, it should look like Figure 2-8.

10. Close the file and the browser.

more

Paragraph, Line Break, or Preformatted Text tags are necessary to create spacing in your Web page. If you add the same text as in the exercise but do not use the Paragraph, Line Break, or Preformatted Text tags, your Web page will look like Figure 2-9. ◥ Certain tags do not require you to create a new paragraph. For example, Header tags automatically include paragraph markers.

A closing Paragraph tag, </P>, is not necessary because once you have created a paragraph, you do not need to end it. You simply start another one. However, you may want to insert it anyway just to maintain the practice of typing opening and closing tags for every command. Furthermore, when you advance to more complex procedures such as using Cascading Style sheets, you will need to close paragraphs to limit a font size, style, or color to that particular paragraph.

Figure 2-7 Paragraphs and spacing in an HTML document

Paragraph tag

Line Break tags

Figure 2-8 Paragraphs and line breaks displayed in a browser

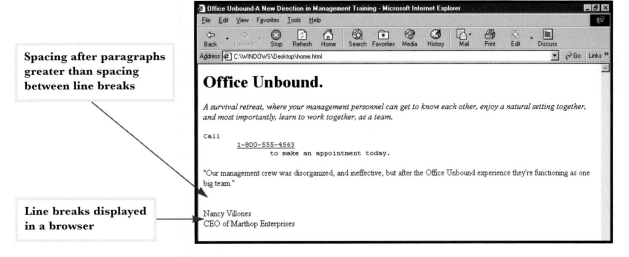

Spacing after paragraphs greater than spacing between line breaks

Line breaks displayed in a browser

Figure 2-9 Spacing improperly displayed

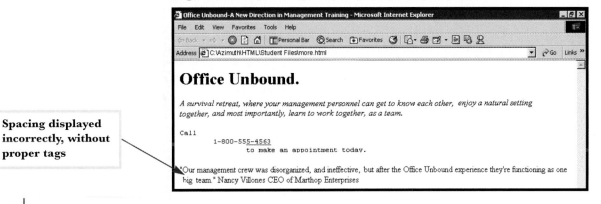

Spacing displayed incorrectly, without proper tags

Practice

Open the title.html file. Add the following list to the document, with a line break between each line of text. The list is: Established 1968, #1 Consumer Choice 5 Years in a row, Top Rated Accountant in the State. Save the file and close it.

skill | Creating Lists

concept

One of the most effective ways to organize information on a Web page is to create a list. HTML instructions include tags for creating several types of lists. You can create a list using preformatted text, but you have more control over the appearance of the list using the list commands. There are three types of lists: Ordered, Unordered and Definition. Ordered or numbered lists are generally used for outlines, sequential steps, or to prioritize information. Unordered or bulleted lists are the most common and are used for any series of items with no particular order. Definition lists are used for glossaries, or any list of words paired with a definition.

do it !

Add a list to an HTML document.

1. Open the document htdoit2-5.txt, from your files. It is the basic structure of an HTML document, with a lot of space between tags.

2. Place the insertion point one line below the opening Head tag. Type: <TITLE>Advantages of a retreat with Office Unbound</TITLE>. Press [Enter] twice.

3. Type: <H3>Advantages of a retreat with Office Unbound</H3>. Place the insertion point one line below the opening Body tag.

4. Type: <UL>, the Unordered List tag. Press [Enter].

5. Type: <LI>, the List Item tag. Then type: A feeling of camaraderie</LI>. Press [Enter].

6. Type the next items, pressing [Enter] after every entry. <LI>Learning to work together</LI>, <LI>Learning to lead a team</LI>, <LI>Learning to compromise</LI>, <LI>Building a common bond</LI>. Press [Enter] after the final entry.

7. Type: </UL>.

8. Click File on the Menu bar, then click Save. Save the file as advantage. Your document should look like Figure 2-10.

9. Click File on the Menu bar, then click Save As. Save the file as advantage.html on your desktop. If you open the Web page in your browser, it should look like Figure 2-11.

10. Close the file and the browser.

more

This is the most complicated tag we have learned thus far as it requires opening and closing tags to mark each list item. The opening tags for an ordered list and a definition list are <OL> and <DL>, respectively. Use the <LI> tag to mark each list item in an ordered list just as you did in the unordered list in the exercise. In a Definition list, each list item is indicated by the tag <DT>, Definition Term, and each definition is tagged <DD>. Definition terms are neither numbered nor bulleted, but the definitions are indented. A Nested list is a list within a list. Create the first list, place the pointer where you want the nested list to appear, and create it in the same way you created the regular list. For example, after <LI>List Item</LI>, type: <OL> to create a nested ordered list.

Using HTML

Figure 2-10 Unordered list in an HTML document

Specifies type of list

List items

Figure 2-11 Unordered list displayed in a browser

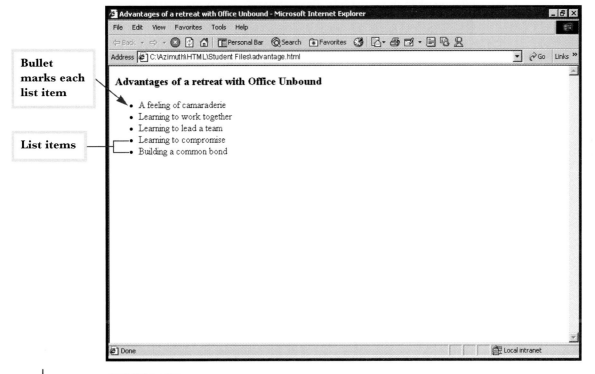

Bullet marks each list item

List items

Practice

Create a new document. Save it as list.html. Create a numbered list of the top ten reasons to see an accountant. Save the file and close it..

skill | Adding and Formatting Tables

concept

Tables are commonly used in Web pages to organize information in a structured and attractive way. They consist of cells formed by the intersection of rows and columns. Creating a table is somewhat complicated because you must divide the information into rows and columns in the HTML source document. It also entails a number of steps, but a table is the perfect way to simplify complicated information. Tables can be created more easily using preformatted text, but you will not be able to add captions, borders, cell spacing or specific formatting to an entire row or column.

do it !

Create a table for the advantage page.

1. Open the advantage document in Notepad.

2. Place the insertion point one line below the closing Unordered List tag. Press [Enter].

3. Type: <TABLE>. Press [Enter]. Type: <TR>, Table Row, to establish that the following items will appear in the same row. Press [Enter].

4. Type: <TH>, the Table Header tag. Then type Plans available:</TH>. Press [Enter]. Type <TD>7 Day Plans</TD>. Press [Enter]. Type: <TD>5 Day Plans</TD>. Press [Enter]. Type: <TD>3 Day Plans</TD>. Press [Enter]. Type <TD>Day Trips Available</TD> </TR>. (Be sure there is no space between the closing </TD> tag and the closing </TR> tag.) Press [Enter] twice.

5. Type <TR>. Press [Enter]. Type <TH>Includes:</TH>. Press [Enter]. Type <TD>Accommodations</TD>. Press [Enter]. Type <TD>Fees</TD>. Press [Enter]. Type <TD>Food</TD>. Press [Enter]. Type <TD>The time of your life</TD></TR>. Press [Enter]. Type </TABLE>. Your table should look like Figure 2-12.

6. To create a border, place the insertion point inside the opening Table tag, after the word TABLE. Press the Space Bar. Type: BORDER. This is an attribute of the table.

7. Type: =3. This is the value for the attribute. It will tell the browser how to display the attribute. Your table should now look like Figure 2-13.

8. Click File on the Menu bar. Click Save.

9. Click File on the Menu bar. Click Save As. Save the file as advantage.html. Click [Yes] to replace the existing file. If you open the Web page in a browser, it will look like Figure 2-14.

10. Close the file and the browser.

more

To place headers in the top row of the table, use a <TH> (Table Header) tag for each item you want to be a header. The <TD> tag is simply used to add cells to a table, the same way the List Item tag adds items to a list. Border thickness is measured in pixels. The table border will be more pronounced as the value for the Border attribute increases.

Figure 2-12 Table created in an HTML document

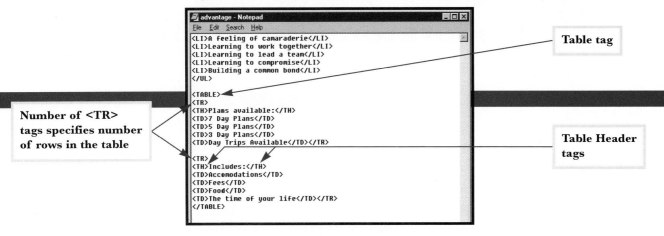

Table tag

Number of <TR> tags specifies number of rows in the table

Table Header tags

Figure 2-13 Attribute in HTML

Attribute

Value

Number of <TD> tags specifies number of cells

Figure 2-14 Table displayed in a browser

Table with specified number of rows and columns

Border appears with specified value

Practice

In the title.html file, add a table with three rows and columns. Add: Don Knobly in the first two cells of the first row. Then add: 452 Debonair Ave. in the three cells in the second row. Then add: Walker, R.I., 57068, in the three cells in the third row. Save the file and close it.

skill | Understanding Anchors

concept

Links can be created to connect to a specific section of a Web page. For example, you can create a link from the top of a page to the bottom of a page. First you will need to create an anchor, which will be referenced when you construct the link. An anchor simply marks a location so that the browser will navigate to it. Anchors are particularly effective for use in lengthy documents. Each section can link back to the Table of Contents. Anchors can be used to construct links within the same document or to a particular area of another Web page. An anchor is created using <A> tags, and the Name attribute. The value for the Name attribute will be the name for the anchor. Some browsers use the term target and anchor synonymously. While they are similar, an anchor on a page is different from the target of a hyperlink.

do it !

Create an anchor and a link to that anchor in an HTML document.

1. Open the file htdoit2-7.txt in Notepad.

2. Scroll down to the last paragraph, or List Item.

3. Place the insertion point after the <LI> tag.

4. Type: <A NAME=MOST>.

5. Place the insertion point at the end of the paragraph, contained within the closing List Item tag.

6. Type: </A>. This will make the entire paragraph the anchor.

7. Scroll up the screen and place the insertion point between the two Head tags.

8. Type: <A HREF=#MOST>Most Important Words</A>.

9. Click File. Click Save As. Save the file as tips.html. Your document should look like Figure 2-15.

10. Open the page in a browser. Your page should look like Figure 2-16.

11. When you move the pointer over Most Important Words, the link in the beginning of the Web page turns into a hand 🖑. If you click on the link, it will take you to the anchor, which is the last List Item.

12. Close the file and the browser.

more

The <A> tag informs the browser that you are creating a link. The HREF attribute stands for Hypertext Reference. If the anchor was in a separate document, such as page.html, you would type: <A HREF= "page. html# anchor name"> to reference the section. Do not put quotes around a Name or HREF value unless the value contains more than one word. If you put quotes around a one-word value, the link will not function properly.

Figure 2-15 Link to an anchor in an HTML document

Hypertext Reference

Value for HREF attribute is the name of the anchor

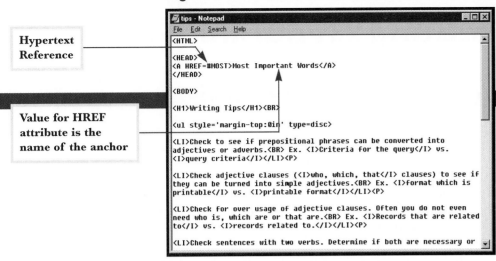

Figure 2-16 Link to an anchor in a browser

Link to an anchor below on the page

Anchor text is below bottom of browser window

Clicking link at top of the page takes you to text containing anchor

Practice

Create an anchor using the last List Item on the list.html file. Create a link to the anchor at the top of the page. Save the file and close it.

skill   Creating Hyperlinks

concept

Hyperlinks are the essence of the World Wide Web. They are pieces of text or images that enable you to jump from page to page within a site or to pages on other sites. A hyperlink connects you to a target or destination document. While an anchor "bookmarks" a particular section of a Web page, a hyperlink connects to the top of the page. Hyperlinks can also be designed to download files, play an audio or video clip, or send e-mail. The value for a hyperlink is the Web page URL.

do it !

Create a hyperlink that links the home page to the advantage page.

1. Open the home document in Notepad.

2. Place the insertion point behind the closing Line Break tag at the bottom of the page.

3. Press [Enter] once.

4. Type: <P><A HREF="advantage.html">Advantages of Coming to Office Unbound</A></P>.

5. Click File on the Menu bar. Click Save. The document should look like Figure 2-17.

6. Click File on the Menu bar. Click Save As. Save the document as home.html.

7. Click [Yes] to replace the existing file.

8. Open the Web page in your browser. This page is shown in Figure 2-18. Scroll to the bottom of the page if necessary.

9. Move the pointer over the hyperlink you created, so that it turns into a hand pointer, ⟨ᵐ⟩.

10. Click on the hyperlink. You will be connected to the advantage Web page.
    Every time you create a link, test the link in the browser to make sure that it works properly. Every link should work when it is clicked in your browser.

11. Close the browser and the file.

more

The process is slightly different to link to another Web site. For example, if you wanted to create a link to the Web site www.domain.website.com, you would type the following tag: <A HREF="http://www.domain.website.com">HYPERLINK</A>. You can also substitute a protocol like ftp: if the address you are linking to does not use HyperText Transfer Protocol. Simply write the location of the address exactly as you would if you were telling your browser to open that page.

In the above exercise you used a relative pathname to specify the location of the advantage.html file. A relative pathname is the "easy way" of specifying a file's location, but only works when the file being referenced is in the same folder as the current document. If it is not, you must use an absolute pathname, which specifies the exact location of the file with more precision.

Figure 2-17 Creating a hyperlink in an HTML document

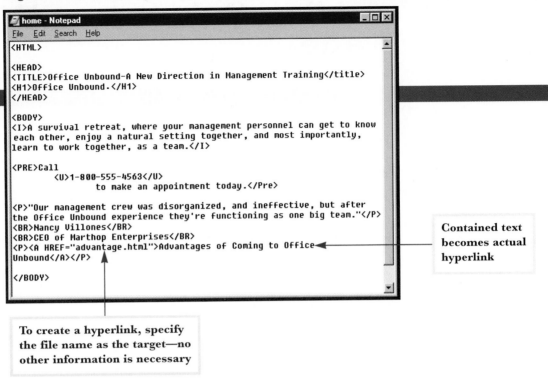

Contained text becomes actual hyperlink

To create a hyperlink, specify the file name as the target—no other information is necessary

Figure 2-18 Hyperlink in a browser

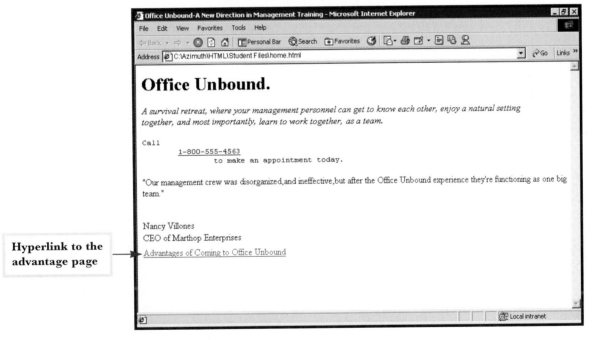

Hyperlink to the advantage page

Practice

Create a link at the bottom of the title.html file to the list.html file you created. Save the file, and make sure the hyperlink works by viewing the page in your browser. Close the browser and the file.

skill Adding Colors to a Web Page

concept

HTML allows you to add background color, and choose colors for text, hyperlinks, tables, borders and more. This enables you to create pages that are attractive and fun. You can set default colors for an entire page or add color individually to objects or text.

do it !

Add a background color and change the text color on the advantage Web page.

1. Open the advantage document in Notepad.

2. Place the insertion point between BODY and the closing angle bracket, >, in the <BODY> tag. Press the [Space Bar].

3. Type: BGCOLOR="#FFFF10". BGCOLOR is the attribute for background color. The value is a Hexadecimal code for a shade of the color yellow.

4. Press the [Space Bar]. Type: TEXT="#299C39". The value is coding for a shade of green. Your document should look like Figure 2-19.

5. Click File on the Menu bar. Click Save.

6. Save the file as advantage.html. Open Web page in your browser. It should look like Figure 2-20.

7. Close the browser and the file.

more

Changing the color of text for a specific object such as a list or a table, or a section of text, is simple. Instead of the Text tag, use the Font tag, Color attribute, and a Hexadecimal value, as follows: <FONT COLOR="#######">. Then, add the closing tag, </FONT>. The text you want to change must be contained within these tags.

There are 16 predefined colors. You do not have to use a Hexadecimal value to use these colors. You may simply use the name of the color. For example, if you wanted to set the default background to the color lime, type: <BODY BGCOLOR="LIME">.

The Hexadecimal system is a complicated way of creating colors on a Web page. The Hexadecimal system uses 16 symbols, 0–9 and A–F. These 16 symbols specify the red, green, and blue components of 255 colors in a base 16 format. The Hexadecimal system is based on the combination of Red, Blue, and Green that make up a particular color. First type: #, then the Hexadecimal combination of six letters and numbers. Lighter colors generally have more letters, and typically begin with the letter F. For example, White is #FFFFFF. Darker colors usually contain more numbers. Black is #000000. Note that Black and White are predefined colors, so you do not need to know their Hexadecimal numbers to use them. In the appendices at the end of this book there is a reference guide that lists the names and color for the 16 predefined colors and their attribute names. It also includes the Hexadecimal code for many common colors.

Figure 2-19 **Color attributes and values in HTML**

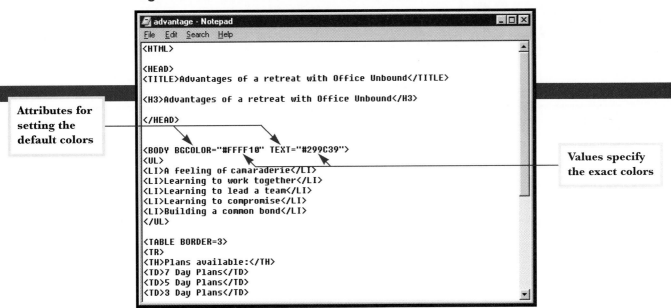

Attributes for setting the default colors

Values specify the exact colors

Figure 2-20 **Color changes viewed in a browser**

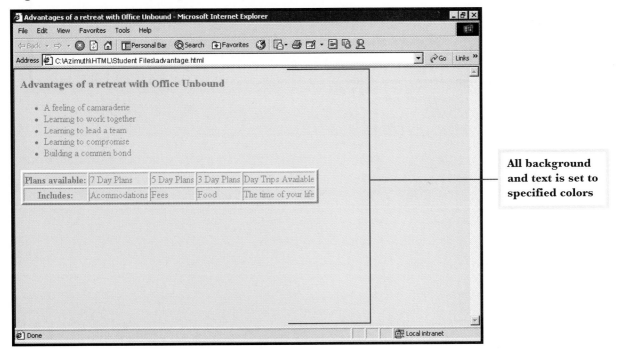

All background and text is set to specified colors

Practice

Change the background color on the list.html file to black, and make the default text color white. Save the file and close it.

shortcuts

HTML Tag	Appearance in Browser (50% of actual size)
<H1>	Heading 1
<H2>	Heading 2
<H3>	Heading 3
<H4>	Heading 4
<H5>	Heading 5
<H6>	Heading 6

A. Identify Key Features

Name the items indicated by callouts in Figure 2-21.

Figure 2-21 An HTML source document

B. Select the Best Answer

10. Appears in the browser, but not in the Web page

11. Text that will appear on a Web page as it appears in the HTML source

12. Tag that identifies a line break

13. Tag that identifies a term definition

14. Tag that identifies a table item

15. A type of system used to add colors on a Web page

16. A location in pages of text that is marked and will later be linked to

17. The destination of a hyperlink

a.

b. <DD>

c. <TD>

d. Anchor

e. Hexadecimal

f. Preformatted

g. Target

h. Title

quiz (continued)

C. Complete the Statement

18. The Title tag is contained within these tags:

a. Body

b. Paragraph

c. Head

d. Table

19. You do not need to use Paragraph tags when you are using Header tags because:

a. Header tags automatically create new paragraphs

b. It will appear in the Web page exactly as it appears on the HTML document

c. Every browser reads and displays HTML the same way

d. Headers and paragraphs are interchangeable

20. If you want to create multiple paragraphs of text without a lot of space in between:

a. Use the Paragraph tag

b. Use the Header tag

c. Use the Ordered list tag

d. Use the Line break tag

21. An Ordered list is also known as a :

a. Bulleted list

b. Numbered list

c. Definition list

d. To Do list

22. To add color to a section of text on a Web page, use:

a. <Text="######">

b. <TXTCOLOR="######">

c. <FONT COLOR="######">

d. <WORD COLOR="######">

23. To add color to a Web page:

a. Use the name of the color and the shade, light or dark

b. Use the Hexadecimal code for the specific color you want

c. Use one of the 31 predefined colors

d. Use the tag <COLOR>

24. The tag <TR> stands for:

a. Tall Roof, for large borders in a table

b. Target Right, for use with hyperlinks

c. Tree, to place a tree diagram on the Web page

d. Table Row, to add a row to a table

interactivity

Build Your Skills

1. Add a title and text to a document:

   a. In Notepad, open the document created on HT1.23, entitled Web Page.

   b. Add a title to the Head section of the document. The title is Sunglass City.

   c. In the Body section of the text, add a Header 3. The Header also reads Sunglass City.

   d. Use the Big tag to format a paragraph of text on your page. The paragraph is Sunglass City where the days are hot and the glasses hotter.

   e. Click File. Click Save As. Save the document as sunglass.html.

2. Add preformatted text to a Web page:

   a. Add this preformatted text to the sunglass page (press [Enter] after each piece of text): Low prices; Huge selection; Discounts; Medical plans accepted; Convenient location.

   b. Resave the sunglass file.

3. Create a list:

   a. Add an Unordered list to the sunglass page.

   b. The list items are: Gargantuas; Tree frogs; Apple eyes; Rose colored; Hunky Dorey; and many others.

   c. Resave the sunglass file.

4. Create a table:

   a. Create a new HTML document in Notepad, beginning with the basic HTML structure. Save the page as prices.html.

   b. Create a table on the prices page. Make sure the table has a border size of 7.

   c. Create three rows, with three Headers. The Headers will be Price range for the first row, Styles for the second row, and Availability for the third row.

   d. The first row will have four table items: $10–25; $30–50; $60–90; and 100 and over.

   e. The second row will have four table items: Men's; Women's; Children's; and Prescriptions.

   f. The third row will have only one table item: All styles subject to availability. Resave the prices file.

5. Create a hyperlink.

   a. Add a hyperlink to the prices page. The hyperlink will appear in the Head section of the document.

   b. Make the link from the prices page to the sunglass page. Resave the prices file.

6. Add color to a Web page:

   a. Change the background color of the sunglass page and the prices page to a light gray. Resave the sunglass file.

   b. Change the color of the data in the table on the prices page to a shade of blue, using this Hexadecimal code: #0000CD (i.e., four zeroes and the letters CD). Resave and close the prices file.

interactivity (continued)

Problem Solving Exercises

1. It's time for you to start working on a Web site for The Fixit Company. Create the Fixit2.html file. First add the title to the page. Create a Header on the page that also says The Fixit Company. You should also include the slogan of the company: Heavy on selection, light on the wallet. Create the following paragraph and format it in bold: We are one of the largest distributors of hardware equipment in the United States, selling to retail outlets, construction companies, and private consumers. Use preformatted text to create a list of locations, pressing [Enter] after each location: Boston, Chicago, Kansas City, Miami, Seattle, San Diego, Houston, and Charlotte. Save the file.

2. Create a new document in Notepad, beginning with the basic HTML structure. Save the page as Options.html. First title the page, The Fixit Company-Payment Options. Then create a Header, Payment Options. Then create a list of payment options. You can use whatever list you think works best. The list items are: Cash, Credit, Cash on delivery, Check, Money order, and Debit. Next, create a table. The table will have two rows. The Header for the first row will be Amount spent, the Header for the second row will be Shipping charge. The table items for the first row are: Less than $100, $101–250, $251–500, $500–$1000. The table items in the second row are: $15, $35, $70, and $150. Below the table create a new paragraph that says: Over $1000 dollars must be special ordered, from 1-800-555-5613. Create one hyperlink from the Fixit2 page to the Options page, then create another hyperlink from the Options page to the Fixit page. Add colors to both pages. Use the references at the end of this book to choose colors for the text and background of these pages. Save the file.

3. Begin creating your own personal Web site. Create a new document and save it as Personal1. Create a title for the document that denotes the subject of the Web site. For example, if you created a soccer Web site, you might title it [Your Name] Soccer Page, or something to that effect. You may want to create a header, although it is not required. Write a paragraph describing the Web site; its purpose, some personal information about yourself, such as your age, where you live, and your education. Format the text in any way you see fit. You may use the formatting tags we used earlier, or preformatted text. Save the file as Personal1.html.

4. Finally, create another page in your personal Web site. Call this new page Index.html. First create a hyperlink that connects from the Index page to your Personal1 page. Then create a hyperlink that connects from your Personal1 page to the Index page. Make a list on the Index page. The list can be of anything related to your topic. For example, if you created a Web site devoted to movies, you might want to list your ten favorite movies. Then, make a table. A table does not have to have Headers; you can simply use them to organize information in an attractive way. Finally, add color to your Web pages. Save both pages.

Advanced HTML Features

You now know the basic principles of HTML, and how to enter and format text, and create anchors and hyperlinks. Congratulations! Now its time to add the sizzle-graphics, images, and other elements that can make a Web page beautiful and exciting.

skills

- ⚡ **Introduction to Web Page Graphics**
- ⚡ **Inserting Images**
- ⚡ **Formatting Images**
- ⚡ **Wrapping Text Around an Image**
- ⚡ **Creating Image Maps**
- ⚡ **Adding Multimedia Files**
- ⚡ **Using Character Tags to Format Text**
- ⚡ **Adding Special Characters to Text**
- ⚡ **Creating an E-mail Link**
- ⚡ **Using Pathnames**

Lesson Goal:

In this lesson, you will learn how to insert and format images and how to wrap text around them. You will also learn how to create an image map and how to work with multimedia files including sound, animation, and video. These elements will allow you to begin using your creativity to stamp your Web page with your own unique style.

Next, you will learn how to apply character tags (which enable you to format just a few characters or a few words) and how to code for special characters. Special characters are unusual symbols, foreign language letters, and accents that are not found on a standard keyboard. Finally, you will learn how to create an e-mail link and how to use pathnames.

You will also learn to work with tags that require multiple attributes and values. This might be confusing at first, but once you become familiar with the technique, the process will become clear.

The skills that teach you how to add beautiful and exciting elements are somewhat difficult but will be worth the effort when you are designing sensational Web pages!

skill

Introduction to Web Page Graphics

concept

Text-only pages are not going to capture the imagination of the Web-surfing public. The best way to add some pizzazz to your pages is to insert images. Images can display or explain information in a lively eye-catching manner.

Adding images is fairly easy. The tag is <IMG SRC="file">. The source attribute simply designates the location of the image. The HTML image formatting options are slightly more difficult to construct.

When you add an image to a Web page, it is not actually part of the document. The image tags tell the browser where to find the image and how to display it. For this reason, you must make sure that the image file name is correct, and that the image is located in the same folder or location as the Web page. This method of accessing an image is known as "inline". An inline image is displayed with a Web page. An external image, on the other hand, must be downloaded separately. Sometimes a miniature version or an icon serves as a hyperlink that leads the visitor to the full-size version.

The most important factor to consider when inserting images is file size. The larger a Web page is, the more memory it requires, and the longer it will take to download. Resist the temptation to add too many images, as each one will increase page-loading time. Several image formats reduce file size and are supported by most browsers.

Most browsers support Graphic Interchange Format (GIF). It is relatively small and is sufficient for low-resolution images. For larger, more color intensive images, the Joint Photographic Experts Group (JPEG) format should be used. Most browsers also support JPEG. GIF and JPEG are the two most common image formats used on the Internet. The GIF format is sufficient for logos, banners and other computer generated art. JPEG should be used for photographs and images with more than 256 colors.

Before you insert an image, you should format it in an image editor such as Adobe Photoshop, Image Edit, or Paint Shop Pro. Image editors allow you to resize, reduce the number of image colors, compress, and save images as JPEG or GIF files. These procedures will help keep download time to a minimum. Photographs can be saved using JPEG compression to retain satisfactory quality while achieving a file size that will not take forever to load.

In this lesson, you will learn how to add an image to your Web page and how to apply some of the available formatting options. You will also learn how to turn your image into a multiple hyperlink called an image map.

Figure 3-1 displays NASA's Earth Observatory Web page, which contains both GIF and JPEG images.

Figure 3-1 NASA Earth Observatory Web page in browser

GIF images

JPEG image

JPEG images

skill | Inserting Images

concept

After you have saved an image in a manageable size and the appropriate format, use the Image tag and the Source attribute to insert it onto your Web page. These commands instruct the browser to locate and open the image. As long as you write your tags correctly, and save your images in the same folder as the Web page, you should have no trouble. Take advantage of the creative ways you can design pages with images. For example, you can group several small images together and create hyperlinks to construct a navigation bar for your site.

do it !

Insert an image onto a new page that you will create in Notepad.

1. Navigate to your Student Files folder and open file htdoit3-2.txt in Notepad.

2. Click File. Click Save As. Save the file as locations.

3. Place the insertion point after the </TITLE> tag. Press [Enter].

4. Type: <IMG SRC="Unbound.jpg">. This image is located in the folder where you have stored your Student Files. Make sure you move it to the same folder as your Web pages. When you are inserting an image below text, put the <IMG> tag inside <P> or <BR> tags to place it on a line of its own.

5. Click File. Click Save. Your document should look like Figure 3-2.

6. Click File. Click Save As. Save the file as locations.html. Open the locations page in your browser. It should look like Figure 3-3.

7. Close the browser.

more

An icon such as ☒ will be displayed instead of your image, if you have made a coding error. You should check several things. First, make sure the file name, Unbound.jpg, is written correctly. If any part of the file name is omitted, the browser will not be able to locate the image. Second, make sure the image and the Web page are in the same folder. They must be in the same folder or the browser will not locate the file and the image will not display.

The <IMG> tag does not require a closing tag. Even when you add formatting attributes, a closing tag is not necessary. Browsers will correctly interpret that the formatting options apply to the inline image.

Figure 3-2 Image added in HTML document

Image tag

Source attribute

Image file name

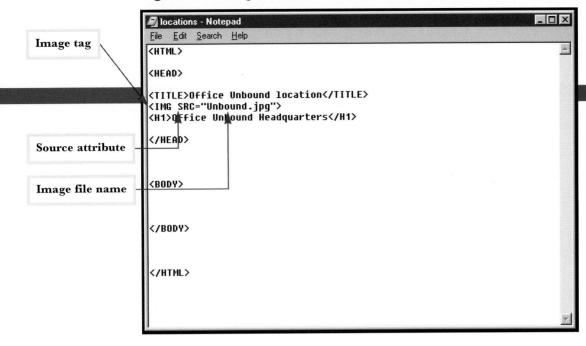

Figure 3-3 Image displayed in a browser

JPEG image

Practice

Add the htprac2.JPG image from the folder where you have stored the Student Files, to the Head section of a new HTML file. Save the file as adimage.html.

skill   Formatting Images

concept

After an image has been added to a Web page, many formatting options are available. You can add a border, or align the image left, right or center. These simple formatting commands are constructed by adding attributes to the Image tag. Borders and image alignment can make your pages more attractive.

do it !

Add a border to an image you have inserted. You will also change the page alignment of the image.

1. Open the locations document in Notepad, if necessary. Place the insertion point between the closing quotation mark, ", and the closing angle bracket, > of the IMG tag. Press the Space Bar.

2. Type: BORDER=5. This attribute will place a border around the image. You can set the Border attribute to BORDER=0 to make sure that no border is inadvertently added to an image.

3. Place the insertion point in front of the opening angle bracket, <, of the IMG tag. Type the HTML tag: <P ALIGN="center">.

4. Place the insertion point after the closing angle bracket, > of the Image tag. Type: </P>.

5. Click File. Click Save. Your file should look like Figure 3-4.

6. Click File. Click Save As. Save the file as locations.html. Click [Yes] to overwrite the existing file. If you open the locations page in a browser, it should look like Figure 3-5.

7. Close the browser.

more

The method used to align the image in the steps above is the same method you would use to align text. Because the image is an inline graphic, it is treated the same as a piece of text, and can therefore be aligned, or have other similar functions performed on it. The higher the value for the Border attribute, the thicker the image border will be. You can also align the image and text to the right, by typing ALIGN="right", and to the left, by typing ALIGN="left".

Figure 3-4 **An image formatted in HTML**

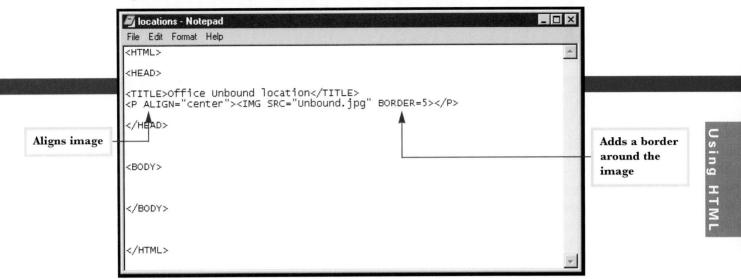

Aligns image

Adds a border
around the
image

Figure 3-5 **Formatted image in a browser**

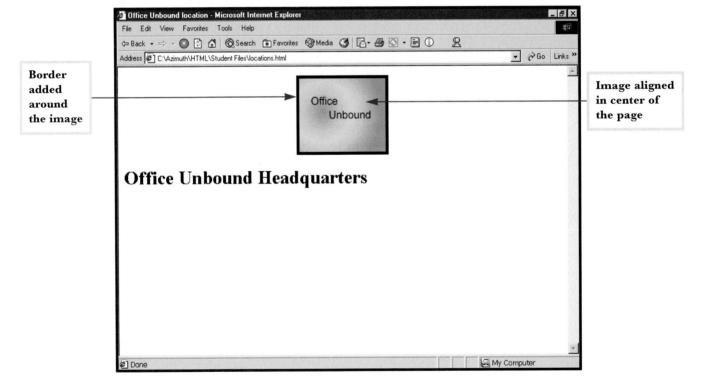

Border
added
around
the image

Image aligned
in center of
the page

Practice

Add a border to the image in the adimage.html file. Set the border thickness to 12. Save the file.

skill | Wrapping Text Around an Image

concept

Text can be wrapped around an image using the Align attribute. Type: ALIGN=left to align the image to the left while the text wraps to the right, or ALIGN=right to align the image to the right while the text wraps on the left. Text wrapping enables text to flow smoothly around logos, digital photographs and other images. Without the text wrapping capability many empty spaces would be left on your Web page.

do it !

Reposition the image to the right, and wrap text around it instead of centering it.

1. In the locations document opened in Notepad, place the insertion point before the opening angle bracket for the Paragraph tag, <. Press [Delete] until the entire Paragraph tag and attributes are deleted.

2. Place the insertion point before the closing Paragraph tag. Press [Delete] until the closing Paragraph tag is deleted.

3. Place the insertion point just to the right of the closing quotation mark of the image source value. Press the Space Bar.

4. Type: ALIGN="right".

5. Place the insertion point on the line below the header, and above the closing Head tag, </HEAD>.

6. Type: <P>A place for people to come together and share an experience. A place for people to work as a team. A place to learn, share, and grow together. Office Unbound is indeed an office unlike any you have ever known. Office Unbound is a unique experience shared.</P>.

7. Type: <BR CLEAR=right>, to stop wrapping the text where there is no longer an image aligned to the right.

8. Click File. Click Save. Your document should look like Figure 3-6.

9. Save the file as locations.html. If you open the locations page in your browser and click the Restore 🔲 button, the page should look like Figure 3-7. ⬤ If the text in your browser window does not wrap around the image as shown, either enlarge the text or shrink the size of the browser window as needed until you achieve the desired effect.

10. Close the browser.

more

To wrap text between two images, first wrap the text around one image, then the other. Insert each image directly before the text that should flow around it. Each image will push the text to one side until there is a break or the text is complete. ⬤ You should make sure not to get confused. You are aligning the image to the right or left, but the text will start wrapping on the opposite side. Also, make sure that you place the image before the text that will wrap around it.

To stop wrapping the text when there is no longer an image aligned on the left, type: <BR CLEAR=left>. To stop a text wrap when you are wrapping text between two images, type: <BR CLEAR=all>.

Using HTML

Figure 3-6 Wrapping text in an HTML document

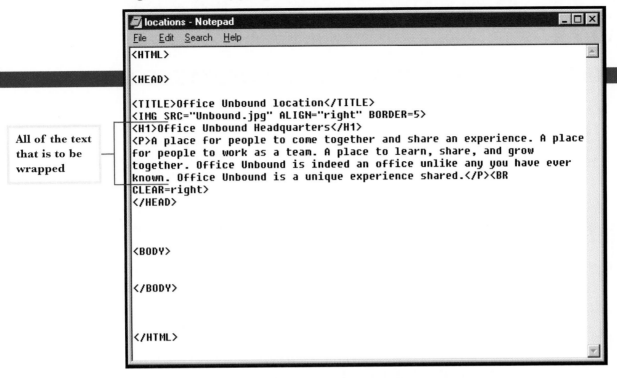

All of the text that is to be wrapped

Figure 3-7 Wrapped text displayed in a browser

Text being wrapped around right-aligned image

Text wrap ends automatically where the image ends

Practice

Keep the image you added earlier to the adimage.html file, aligned to the left. Wrap only the header around it. Save the file.

skill | Creating Image Maps

concept

Images can be ornamental and functional. You can make an image into a single hyperlink, or create multiple hyperlinks on one image. An image map contains any number of areas, also known as hotspots, that when clicked connect you to a different page or section. To create an image map you must specify the pixel coordinates of each hotspot.

do it !

Create links to both the home page and the advantage page from the image on the locations page.

1. Open the locations document in Notepad, if necessary.

2. Place the insertion point between the value 5, for the BORDER attribute, and the closing angle bracket, >. Press Space Bar.

3. Type: USEMAP="#Unbound".

4. Place the insertion point two lines below the closing Head tag. Type the following tag: <MAP NAME="Unbound">. Press [Enter].

5. Type: <AREA SHAPE="rect" COORDS="0,0,85,45" HREF="home.html">. Press [Enter].

6. Type: <AREA SHAPE="rect" COORDS="50,50,148,121" HREF="advantage.html">. Press [Enter]. Type: </MAP>.

7. Click File. Click Save. Your document should look like Figure 3-8.

8. Save the file as locations.html. Open the Locations page in your browser. If you move the pointer over the image it will turn into a hand, 🖑. The upper-left corner of the image, including the word Office links to the home page, and the lower-right corner, including the word Unbound links to the advantage page. Your page should look like Figure 3-9.

9. Close the browser and the locations document.

more

For a rectangular area, coordinates are arranged so that the x, y coordinates for the upper-left corner are first, and the coordinates for the lower-right corner are second (x1, y1, x2, y2). You can make a circular region using the x, y coordinates for the center of the circle and the measurement of the radius, r. A polygonal area is created using coordinates for each point on the polygon (x1, y1, x2, y2, x3, y3) The following attributes create the following geometric shapes: (1) default creates an area covering the entire region, (2) rect creates a rectangular region, (3) circle creates a circular region, and (4) poly creates a polygonal, or many-sided, region.

Open your image in an image editor. When you move the pointer over the image, the pixel coordinates should be displayed. If not, use the Menu bar to open a window that will display the pixel coordinates of your image. This will give you the precise pixel coordinates to use for your hotspots. ◆ If the areas overlap, the browser will usually use the link that was defined first. Do not put your clickable areas too close together or the user could click and go to the wrong page.

Figure 3-8 Image map specified in HTML

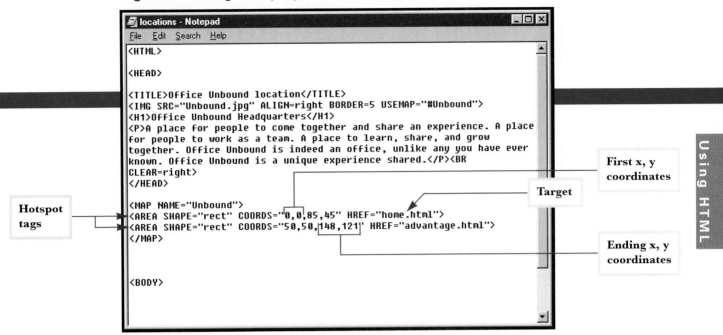

Hotspot tags

First x, y coordinates

Target

Ending x, y coordinates

Figure 3-9 Image map in a browser

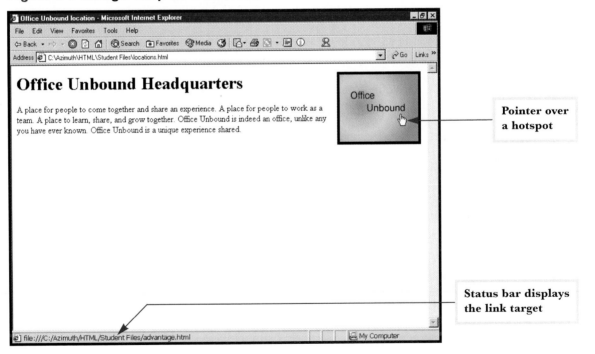

Pointer over a hotspot

Status bar displays the link target

Practice

Create an image map using the image on the adimage.html file. Make the hotspot with whatever dimensions you would like. Create another HTML file and name it Top Ten.html. Link the image on the adimage.html file to the Top Ten page. Save the files and close the adimage.html file.

skill

Adding Multimedia Files

concept

The popularity of the Web has been fueled by the development of audio and video files and animations. The disadvantage of multimedia files is that they are often large, external files, which can take a long time to download. However, inline movies in AVI format and animated GIFs can be added to a Web page and played automatically. These files are collectively called multimedia files.

do it !

Add a small piece of animation to the home page.

1. Open the home document in Notepad.

2. Place the insertion point after the opening Head tag.

3. Press [Enter].

4. Type: <IMG SRC=compass.gif>. Make sure your link to an external file includes information such as file size and format so users can decide whether or not to download it.

5. Click File. Click Save. Your document should look like Figure 3-10.

6. Save the document as home.html.

7. Open the home page in your browser. It should look like Figure 3-11.

8. Close the browser.

more

The method described above is for adding an inline multimedia file. Internet Explorer allows you to add a background sound that plays automatically. The tag is <BGSOUND SRC="sound.ext"> (file name and extension). Netscape has a Live Audio plug-in that visitors can operate using Play, Stop and Volume control buttons. The <EMBED SRC="sound.ext"> tag instructs the browser to play the sound in the Web page itself. A plug-in is an enhancement added to a program to perform a specific function.

One way to deal with large audio and video files is to keep them external and create a link. The link can be an icon, picture or descriptive piece of text. Make the destination target the external multimedia file. Your page will load quickly and the visitor can decide whether or not to wait to access the file. For example, in Netscape, you can use the tag, <A HREF="sound.ext"> (the location and extension of the file) to allow visitors to choose whether or not to access large audio files.

Just like images, multimedia files and the Web page associated with them, must be kept in the same folder. The browser will not be able to locate the inline file, or link to the external file, if you neglect to do this.

Figure 3-10 Animation inserted in HTML

The animation is saved as a GIF file, and treated as an image

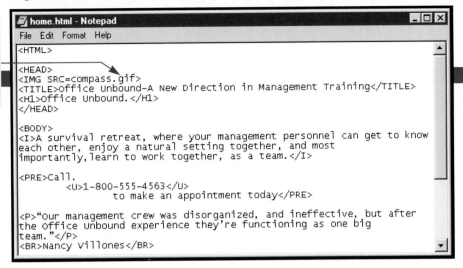

Figure 3-11 Animation displayed in a browser

Animation appears whenever the Web page is opened

Practice

Create a link on the Top Ten page. The link should be, "Can I help you?"(20.2kb). Link this to the file Sound3.wav present in the folder where you have stored your Student Files. After the link, write text that says, This is Don Knobly's secretary Lisa Wessly. Open the Top Ten page in your Web browser, and click on the link to play the .wav file. If necessary, follow any additional on-screen prompts in order to play the file.

skill | Using Character Tags to Format Text

concept

A particularly effective way to emphasize a section of text is to apply character tags to several characters or words. You have already learned several character tags: <BIG>, <B> (bold) and <I> (italic). Other character tags, such as the subscript and superscript tags, are useful for certain abbreviations and for mathematical and scientific formulas. The <CODE> tag can be used to create a mono-spaced font for URLs, computer code, and other text you want to offset from the main text. Internet Explorer even supports the <BLINK> tag with which you can emphasize a pertinent word, or a hyperlink. ⬤ Character tags are so named because rather than affecting the entire document, or an object in the document, they can be used on individual characters.

do it !

Use character tags to format text on the home page.

1. Open the home document in Notepad, if necessary. Place the insertion point after the opening tag for the hyperlink at the bottom of the page.

2. Type: <EM><STRONG>. The <EM> tag stands for emphasizing and generally applies italics. The <STRONG> tag displays bold text.

3. Place the insertion point after Unbound.

4. Type: </STRONG></EM>.

5. Click File. Click Save. Your document should look like Figure 3-12.

6. Save the file as home.html. If you open the page in your browser it should look like Figure 3-13. Close the browser.

more

There are two types of character tags, logical and physical. Logical character tags specify how you want to use the text rather than how to display it. The browser decides how to display the text. Physical tags allow you to specify exactly what format changes you want the browser to display. For example, <STRONG> and <EM> are logical tags because while they tell browsers that you want to emphasize text, the browser decides how to emphasize it. The <B> and <I> tags are physical tags because they tell the browser to display bold and italics.

As you saw in the do it! section, you can add character tags to hyperlinks. The default hyperlink color is blue, but you can change the color of links that have not been visited using LINK=. Use VLINK= to change the color of visited links and ALINK= to change hyperlink color when a visitor clicks it. After the equal sign, enter the hexadecimal code or one of the 16 predefined colors.

Figure 3-12 Character tags added to the HTML document

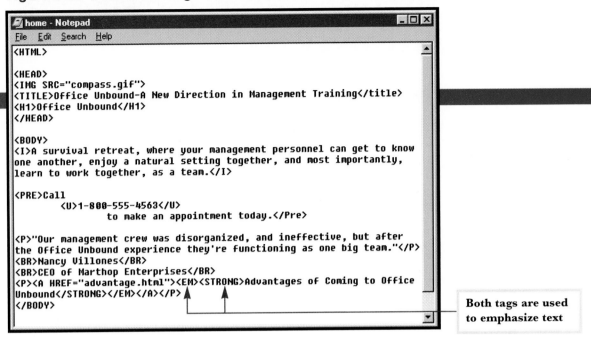

Both tags are used to emphasize text

Figure 3-13 Character tags applied in a browser

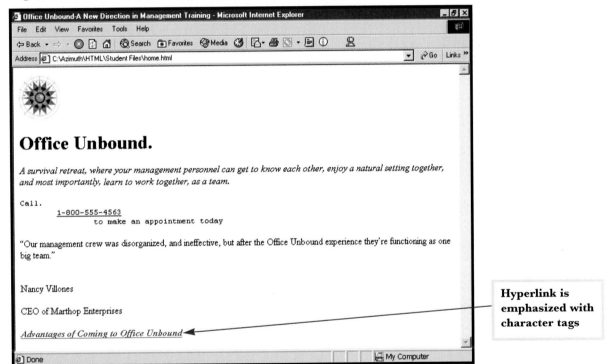

Hyperlink is emphasized with character tags

Practice

Use one of the character tags you learned on the previous page to format six list items on the Top Ten page. Save the file and close it.

skill · Adding Special Characters to Text

concept

You can create special characters such as accented and other foreign letters, dollar and cent signs, the ampersand (&), ellipsis (...), number (#) and at (@) symbols, using HTML code. The copyright, registered, and trademark symbols can also be inserted. These symbols are coded using the ampersand followed by the # sign and a number between 127 and 255.

do it !

Add the registered mark symbol to the name of the company in the Head section of the Home page.

1. Open the home document in Notepad, if necessary.

2. Place the insertion point between Unbound and the </H1> tag.

3. Type: ®. This is the code for the registered mark symbol.

4. Click File. Click Save. Your document should look like Figure 3-14.

5. Save the document as home.html. Open the home page in your browser. The page should look like Figure 3-15.

6. Close the browser.

more

Typing &, followed by #, alerts the browser that what follows is a special character. Some other common special characters are the greater than (>) and less than (<) symbols and the percent (%) sign. Many special characters are foreign letters, which can prove useful in certain instances. For example, the occasion may arise where you need the Spanish "tilde" or the French "accent grave" to correctly spell a proper name. A math teacher may need Greek letters to write formulas for an online class or a "homework help" page. HTML special characters enable you to accomplish these tasks. Some special characters have name codes that make it easier to add them. Use the appendix at the end of this book to view the list of special characters and their name codes.

Figure 3-14 Special character code in an HTML document

Special character code requires no tags or attributes

Figure 3-15 Special character in a browser

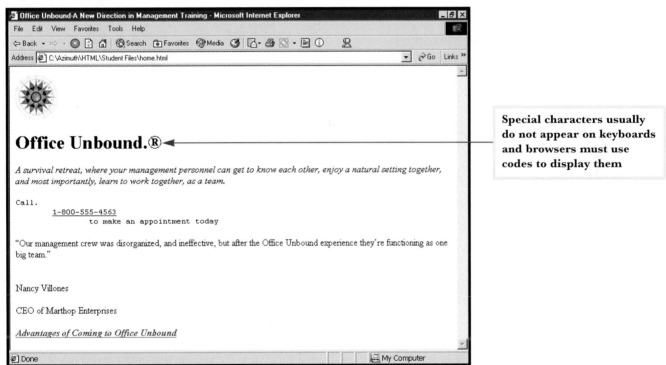

Special characters usually do not appear on keyboards and browsers must use codes to display them

Practice

Place the code © and type: the date in the last line before the closing Body tag on the adimage.html file. Save the file.

skill | Creating an E-mail Link

concept

You can create links that allow a user to send electronic mail (e-mail) to a specified address. E-mail links to the Webmaster—generally the creator and/or manager of a site—are common. E-mail links can also be used to request information, contact key company personnel, or inquire about services. When the users click the link, their browser's e-mail program opens to a mail composing window with the specified address already inserted.　E-mail links are not standard HTML. Although no browser claims to support them, they work in both Internet Explorer and Netscape Navigator.

do it !

Create a link that allows visitors to e-mail Office Unbound.

1. Open the home document in Notepad, if necessary.

2. Place the insertion point after the closing EM, Strong, and Paragraph tags at the bottom of the page. Press [Enter].

3. Type: <A HREF="mailto:info@officeunbound.domain.com">E-mail us for more information</A>. Press [Enter].

4. Click File. Click Save. Your document should look like Figure 3-16.

5. Save the document as home.html. Open the Home page in your browser. Your screen will look like Figure 3-17.

6. Close the browser.

more

You can also link to a newsgroup. To create a link to a newsgroup, type the HTML tag: <A HREF="news:newsgroup.group">. This link will allow the visitors to link to the specified newsgroup the same way they can link to an e-mail address or link to another Web page document.

Often a good way to indicate that a link goes to an e-mail address is to make the e-mail address the actual link. For example, type: <A HREF="mailto:name@server.net">name@server.net</A>. This will create a link that is exactly the same as the e-mail address.

Figure 3-16 Link to e-mail in an HTML document

Figure 3-17 An e-mail link to a mail program

HTML link
to an e-mail
address

E-mail link
in a web page

Practice

Create a link at the bottom of the adimage.html file, that says, E-mail Don Knobly. The e-mail address is DKnobly@personalaccount.domain.com. Save the file and close it.

skill

Using Pathnames

concept

Pathnames are used to specify the location of a file and identify the path that will be taken to find the file. The path to some files can be quite complex, for instance, in a subfolder of a subfolder of a folder. In the Windows environment, for example, a pathname such as C:\ProgramFiles\ Accessories\MSpaint would refer to the C: drive on a computer (usually the hard drive), the Program Files folder stored on the C: drive, the Accessories subfolder stored in the Program Files folder, and then the Microsoft Paint program file within the Accessories subfolder.

To create links or insert images or multimedia files, you will need to know their pathnames. If you do not formulate the pathname correctly, the browser will be unable to locate the image or page. You will end up with images that do not display and hyperlinks that do not function.

There are two types of pathnames, relative and absolute. Relative pathnames do not specify the exact location (i.e., what folders a file is in). Instead, they describe where a file is in relation to the current location (where the file is from here). In order for a relative pathname to work, the file being referenced must be in the same folder as the present location. The relative pathname for a file in the same folder will simply be the file name and extension ("sound.wav"). For a file that is in a subfolder inside the current folder, the pathname will be the subfolder name followed by a forward slash, /, and then the file name and extension (sounds/sound.wav).

If you use an absolute pathname, the files do not have to be in the same folder. An absolute pathname specifies the exact location, or address, of a file. Absolute pathnames have no relationship to the current location. The advantage to using absolute pathnames is that they do not change as long as you do not move a file (e.g., a permanent address). Absolute pathnames must be used for newsgroups, e-mail links and any file that does not use HTTP (Hypertext Transfer Protocol). The disadvantage is that they can be long and tedious to type. You should use relative pathnames whenever possible because they are short; thus there is less chance of making an error. As long as the relative position of each file stays the same, your images will be located and your links will work.

To locate a link, image, or other file that you would like to use in an HTML document with relative pathnames, you must first ensure that the HTML document and the file you want to use are located in the same folder. Relative pathnames are generally used for hyperlinks and linking to other documents on your Web pages.

To find the absolute pathname of a file, use Windows Explorer. Use the View menu to open the Toolbar submenu. Be sure that the Standard Buttons bar and Address bar are activated. (Activated toolbars have a check mark next to their names on the submenu.) A portion of the absolute pathname of any file you want to use will display in the Address bar at the top of the screen, as shown in Figure 3-18. Select the partial absolute pathname, and copy it into your HTML document. Be sure to enter the filename at the end of the partial absolute pathname to make it a complete pathname. Pathnames actually become URLs when the pages are published. For example, relative pathnames will be the URLs the browser will use to locate and open your Web pages and images.

Figure 3-18 The absolute pathname to locate Internet Explorer

Path taken to locate files ("C" hard drive, Program Files folder, and Internet Explorer subfolder)

File located within the Internet Explorer subfolder

shortcuts

Tag	Function	Logical/Physical
<B>	Makes text bold	physical
<BIG>	Displays text in a big font	physical
<CITE>	A short citation or quotation	logical
<CODE>	Indicates text should be displayed in a monospaced font	logical
<EM>	Emphasizes text, usually by italicizing it	logical
<I>	Italicizes text	physical
<KBD>	Specifies keyboard text	logical
<SMALL>	Displays text in a small font	physical
<STRONG>	Emphasizes text, usually bolding it	logical
<SUB>	Displays text as subscript	physical
<SUP>	Displays text as superscript	physical
<TT>	Displays font with same width for each character	physical
<VAR>	Displays a variable, often italicized or underlined	logical

A. Identify Key Features

Name the items indicated by callouts in Figure 3-19.

Figure 3-19 Advanced features in an HTML document

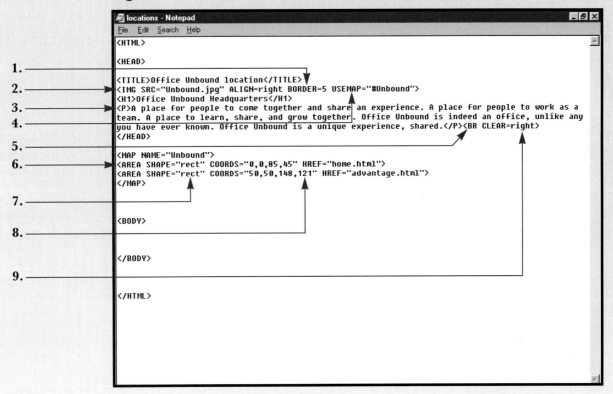

B. Select the Best Answer

10. Does not require a closing tag

11. Coordinates for a circle are listed this way

12. Use this attribute to center an image

13. A type of multimedia file

14. One of the most common file types for saving images

15. Formats text based on how text is used

16. Formats characters exactly as you want them to look

17. Formats characters

18. Adds characters you can't add from a keyboard

a. ALIGN

b. JPEG

c. Logical tags

d. Image tag

e. Physical tags

f. Character tags

g. Sound

h. x, y, r

i. Special characters

quiz (continued)

C. Complete the Statement

19. An image that is displayed with a Web page without being downloaded separately is called:

a. A multimedia file

b. An inline image

c. An image map

d. An animation

20. When you insert an image, this attribute is the one that tells the browser where to find the image:

a. IMG

b. BORDER

c. USEMAP

d. SRC

21. To completely erase the border around an image, the value of the BORDER attribute should be:

a. 0

b. 1

c. 3

d. NONE

22. To wrap text around the right side of an image, the Image attribute and value should be:

a. ALIGN=right

b. ALIGN=left

c. ALIGN=center

d. ALIGN=justify

23. If the coordinates for a hotspot are 12, 12, 43, 55, 123, 77, the shape of the hotspot is:

a. A circle

b. A rectangle

c. A polygon

d. An ellipse

24. An image which you want to insert has a very large file size. You should:

a. Only send it by request to people who e-mail you

b. Add it directly to the Web page

c. Create a link on the page that connects directly to the file

d. Cut it into multiple pieces and only display it a piece at a time

25. Type this first so that browsers can decipher the special character code which follows:

a. @

b. &

c. #

d. %

interactivity

Build Your Skills

1. Insert and format an image:

   a. In Notepad, open the sunglass document that you created in Lesson 2.

   b. Insert the image htskills3-1.jpg into the body of the document.

   c. Set the border for the image at 3.

   d. Wrap the text that appears contained in a <BIG> tag around the right side of the image.

   e. Save the sunglass document.

2. Create an image map:

   a. Use the AREA SHAPE tag and circ attribute to create a circular hotspot on the image that you just inserted. The USEMAP name is logo.

   b. The coordinates are 85, 68, 40. Link the hotspot to the Prices page.

   c. Save the sunglass document. Save it again as sunglass.html. Move the pointer over the image to find the hotspot. Test it to make sure it works.

3. Use character tags and special characters:

   a. Add two special characters to the sunglass page. First add a registered mark symbol after the name of the company, Sunglass City. Then add a copyright symbol and the date at the bottom of the page. Use the reference guide in the appendix to find the proper codes.

   b. Save the sunglass document.

4. Create an e-mail link:

   a. At the bottom of the sunglass page, create a link to the e-mail address Greg@sunglasscity.domain/ceo.com. The link should be the same as the e-mail address.

   b. Save the sunglass document.

interactivity (continued)

Problem Solving Exercises

1. Excellent job! The executives at The Fixit Company are happy with your work. Now, it is time to enhance the Web site using some of the more advanced features of HTML. Open the fixit2.html document from Lesson 2 and save it as fixit3.html. First you must add an image to the Web site. This should be a logo you design yourself, but if you have access to an appropriate photo, you may use that instead. Make sure that you save the logo as a GIF or JPEG. Place the image on the top-left side of the page. Also create an image map. Use a shape and coordinates that conform to an area on your image, and link the area to the Options page. If you have access to an appropriate video, animation, or sound file, insert it into the Fixit page. (You can find many images, photos, sounds, and motion clips at Microsoft's Design Gallery Live at http://dgl.microsoft.com on the Internet.) However, the executives at The Fixit Company do not want the page to take a long time to download, so keep that in mind. Finally, save the document as fixit3.html.

2. Open The Fixit Company's options.html file from Lesson 2 and save it as options3.html. First, use character tags to format the payment options list. Apply the <STRONG> tag to emphasize the list items. Next, use the special character code, &#36, to add the dollar sign to the appropriate table items. Format the final paragraph, which contains the phone number, using the <SMALL> tags. Finally, create an e-mail link at the bottom of the page. Make the e-mail address: info@fixit.domain.com, the link. Add a copyright symbol and the date below the e-mail link. Use the reference guide in the appendix to find the correct code. Save the document as options3.html.

3. Open the personal1.html file from Lesson 2 and save it as personal3.html. It is time to use advanced HTML features to format your Web site. Take out your plans, outline, and list of favorite elements. First, decide what images to use. You may publish images that you create yourself, but if you use other people's work, you must get copyright permission. Format the image to enhance the visual appeal of your site. Design your page layout, determining where the image would look best and if you should wrap text around it. Create as many pages as you want. Then, design your site structure, and link the pages together. When you are finished, save your document as personal3.html.

4. Several more elements should be added to the personal3.html file. At the bottom of the page, add an e-mail link. The target destination should be your own e-mail address. Make the label anything you want. It can be a piece of text, your e-mail address, an image, or simply your name. Use character tags to format some text on each of these two pages. You may want to emphasize something, apply italics, or use a subscript or superscript. If necessary, use special character codes to apply dollar or cent signs, or insert a trademark, copyright or registered symbol. When all of your formatting changes are complete, resave the document as personal3.html.

Creating Forms and Publishing Web Pages

Have you ever purchased a product on the Internet? Participated in a survey? Entered a contest or registered for a site? All of these experiences are interactive. Communication is a two-sided affair. So far in this book, we have concentrated on effective and engaging ways to communicate your ideas to others. This lesson will teach you how your Web site visitors can communicate with you. Forms help to make the Web a dynamic interactive experience.

Forms enable visitors to submit information back to a Web site. They contain data entry fields called input fields or controls. There are two parts to a form: the form structure, consisting of the data entry fields, labels and buttons; and the processing script, or application, which converts the submitted information into a usable format.

≶ **Using Forms**

≶ **Adding Text Entry Fields**

≶ **Inserting Check Boxes and Option Buttons**

≶ **Creating List Menus and Scroll Boxes**

≶ **Adding Command Buttons to a Form**

≶ **Sending Information from a Form**

≶ **Directing Visitors to a Web Site**

≶ **Publishing Web Pages**

Lesson Goal:

In this lesson, you will learn how to create the controls—text entry boxes, option buttons, check boxes, list menus, command buttons and scroll boxes—that visitors will use to answer questions or provide information. You will learn which input fields are most efficient for various question types and how to formulate the HTML commands to construct them. You will also become familiar with the concepts and terminology, and learn a simple method for submitting unprocessed forms to your own e-mail address. Next, you will learn how to register keywords with a search engine, so that visitors can find your page. Finally, you will be given some helpful hints on Web site publishing.

skill | Using Forms

concept

You can use forms on your Web site to take orders for goods and services, conduct surveys, get visitor feedback, register visitors, and many other activities. Visitors can respond to your requests for information by easily filling in text boxes, clicking option buttons, using list menus, or scrolling lists. Forms make information gathering simple and highly efficient.

If you have surfed the Web to any extent, you are probably familiar with the various controls we will create in this lesson. Text entry boxes typically contain one line of text and are used in situations where the information will be unique to each individual user, such as name, user ID or password. Option buttons and check boxes limit the type of information a visitor can enter. Several options are presented from which the user must choose. List menus and scroll boxes present lists of possible answers. They are generally used in situations where there are many choices.

The two command buttons common to all forms are the Submit and Reset buttons. The Submit button sends the information to the server. The Reset button enables the user to start over with a new form set to the default values you have designated. You may be familiar with other command buttons such as the Log On and Log Off buttons present on some Web sites.

Processing forms generally requires a simple application called a CGI (Common Gateway Interface) script to work. This program communicates with the server to take the information submitted by visitors and send it back to the Web site in a readable format. Your ISP (Internet Service Provider) may or may not allow you to run a CGI script for security reasons. However, there are form-hosting services that will process your forms and e-mail the collated results back to you, at no charge, if you allow them to run a banner ad on your form page. CGI scripts are generally written in a programming language called PERL. However if you don't know PERL, there are many ready-to-use CGI scripts available on the Web.

In this lesson we will show you how to format the HTML instructions that will submit each form individually to your e-mail address. You will receive them in an unprocessed format. Each submission will consist of name-value pairs corresponding to the controls you have created for the form. For example, name=smith &email=smith @aol.com &payment=Visa. This method will suffice for personal Web sites where your respondents will be few. You will be able to interpret and collate the information yourself, but business sites will require a CGI script on a server, or a form-hosting service.

Figure 4-1 displays a guest book form from the NASA Web site that includes text entry fields and command buttons.

Figure 4-2 displays the HTML code for the guest book page form shown in Figure 4-1. It includes some of the tags you will be learning in this lesson, and shows you how your HTML document may look when you create a form.

Figure 4-1 A guestbook form in a browser

Text entry fields

Two command buttons: one submits information, one resets the form

Figure 4-2 HTML source of guestbook

Code for text entry field

Code for command buttons

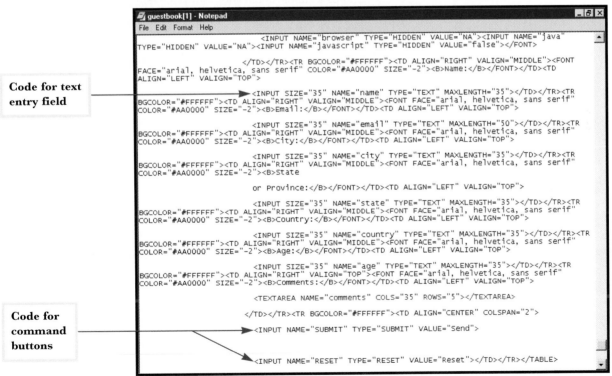

skill | Adding Text Entry Fields

concept

Text entry fields are text boxes that allow users to enter information. You can specify the size and type of a text entry field when you are creating it. Text entry fields are typically used to collect names, addresses, credit card numbers and other information that is unique to the visitor.

do it !

Create a form and add text entry fields to collect information for Office Unbound.

1. Open the htdoit4-2.txt file in Notepad.

2. Click File. Click Save As. Save the document as form.txt, in the folder where you have saved the student files.

3. Place the insertion point two lines below the opening Body tag.

4. Type: <FORM>. Press [Enter].

5. Type: <P>Name: <INPUT TYPE="TEXT" SIZE=27 NAME="name"></P>. Press [Enter]
   To create a password box, enter Password as the Input Type. All other attributes can be the same. When the visitor fills in the field, bullets or asterisks will hide the letters, depending on which browser you are using.

6. Type: <P>Address: <INPUT TYPE="TEXT" SIZE=25 NAME="address"></P>. Press [Enter].

7. Type: <P>City: <INPUT TYPE="TEXT" SIZE=28 NAME="city">. Press [Enter].

8. Type: State: <INPUT TYPE="TEXT" SIZE=2 NAME="state">. Press [Enter].

9. Type: Zip Code: <INPUT TYPE="TEXT" SIZE=5 NAME="zip"></P>. Press [Enter].

10. Type: </FORM>.

11. Click File. Click Save. The document should look like Figure 4-3.

12. Click File, click Save As. Save the file as form.html. If you open the page in your browser, it should look like Figure 4-4.

13. Close the browser and the file.

more

The value for text box size is measured in characters. Characters include letters and spaces. The size attribute limits the number of characters that may be entered into the field. For example, setting the State field to 2 limits users to entering the state abbreviation. The default size for a text box in HTML is 20 characters.

If you want to create a large text box, use the tag <TEXTAREA>. Add the attributes NAME, ROWS = the number of rows in the text box, COLS = the number of columns, and WRAP to keep the text within the margins.

Figure 4-3 A form added to an HTML document

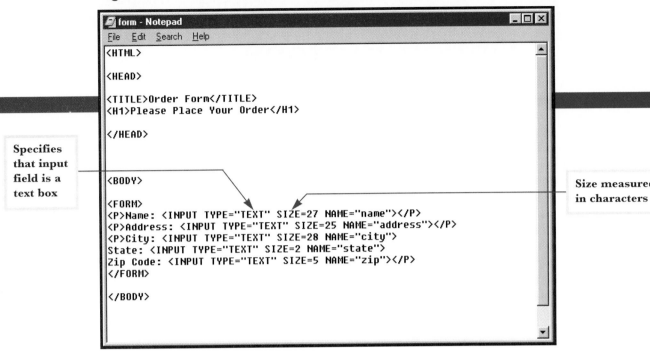

Specifies that input field is a text box

Size measured in characters

Figure 4-4 Text boxes in a browser

Paragraph spacing can be used to organize form

Practice

Begin by creating a new document. Write the basic HTML structure, then create a form that contains the text entry fields user's name, phone number, address, city, state, and annual income. Save the document as account.

skill
Inserting Check Boxes and Option Buttons

concept

Check boxes and option buttons are similar in that they limit visitors to one or more options. Option buttons offer a group of options from which only one can be chosen. Check boxes are often used to answer yes or no questions, but can also be created in situations where you want to allow multiple selections. A set of check boxes can be presented from which the user checks all answers that apply. Both input fields facilitate data entry by allowing visitors to answer questions with a few clicks of the mouse.

do it !

Add some check boxes and some option buttons to the form page.

1. Open the form document in Notepad. Place the insertion point after the final closing Paragraph tag. Press [Enter] twice.

2. Type: <P>Please choose a payment method:</P>. Press [Enter].

3. Type: <INPUT TYPE="RADIO" NAME="payment" VALUE="credit">Credit. Press [Enter]. Type: <INPUT TYPE="RADIO" NAME="payment" VALUE="debit">Debit. Press [Enter]. Type: <INPUT TYPE="RADIO" NAME="payment" VALUE="check">Check. Press [Enter] twice. Check boxes and option buttons are linked in a group by the NAME attribute. It identifies them as members of a particular set. This allows multiple sets of boxes or buttons to occupy one form without confusing data analysis. The INPUT TYPE tag uses the word "radio" to identify option buttons because they resemble the round push buttons on car radios.

4. Type: <P>You may check more than one:</P>. Press [Enter]. Type: <P>Why would you like to attend Office Unbound?</P>. Press [Enter].

5. Type: <INPUT TYPE="CHECKBOX" NAME="attend" VALUE="fun">Fun. Press [Enter]. Type: <INPUT TYPE="CHECKBOX" NAME="attend" VALUE="learn">Learn survival techniques. Press [Enter]. Type: <INPUT TYPE="CHECKBOX" NAME="attend" VALUE="meet">Meet new people. Press [Enter]. Type: <INPUT TYPE="CHECKBOX" NAME="attend" VALUE="know">Know my coworkers better. Press [Enter] twice.

6. Click File. Click Save. Your document should look like Figure 4-5.

7. Click File. Click Save As. Save the file as form.html. Click [Yes] to overwrite the existing file. If you open your page in your browser, it should look like Figure 4-6.

8. Close the browser.

more

Keyboard shortcuts can be created for option buttons and check boxes. Inside the Input Type tag, add the attribute ACCESSKEY=a, where "a" represents any letter of the alphabet. Add (Alt–A) or (ALT+A) next to the text box label to let visitors know that keyboard shortcuts are available. You can create a keyboard shortcut for each check box in a set.

Figure 4-5 Option buttons and check boxes in an HTML document

Tag used to create option buttons

Tag used to create check boxes

Figure 4-6 Option buttons and check boxes in a browser

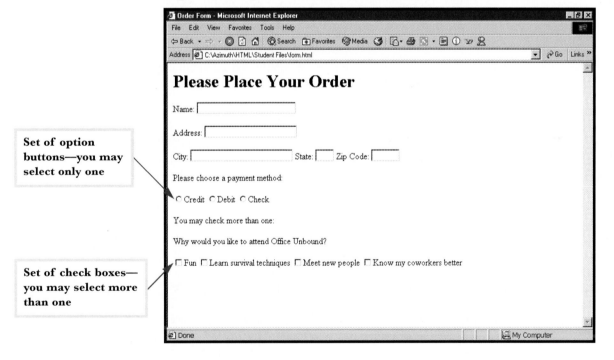

Set of option buttons—you may select only one

Set of check boxes—you may select more than one

Practice

Create a new HTML file. Create a group of option buttons in this file for which the text is, How did you hear about us? The buttons should read Newspaper, The Web, and Word of mouth. Then add one check box, with the text, Have we served you before? Save the file as pracform.html.

skill   Creating List Menus and Scroll Boxes

concept

List menus save space on your form when there are many choices. A set of ten check boxes or option buttons would occupy considerable space. A list menu will display its list of options only when the user clicks an arrow to open the menu. A scroll box displays more than one item at a time and the user scrolls through to uncover the remaining options. Both the input fields make it easy for visitors to answer questions or furnish search criteria.

do it !

Add a list menu and a scroll box to the form page.

1. Place the insertion point after the word better. Press [Enter] twice.

2. Type: <P>How long will you be staying?</P>. Press [Enter]. Type: <SELECT NAME="staying">. Press [Enter]. Type: <OPTION SELECTED VALUE="weekend">Weekend. Press [Enter]. Type: <OPTION VALUE="3">3 Days. Press [Enter]. Type: <OPTION VALUE="5">5 Days. Press [Enter]. Type: <OPTION VALUE="7">1 Week. Press [Enter]. Type: </SELECT>.

3. Press [Enter] twice.

4. Type: <P>You may select more than one option. (Hold down the [CTRL] key while click-ing desired options.):</P>. Press [Enter]. Type: <P>During which month(s) would you like to visit?</P>. Press [Enter].

5. Type: <SELECT NAME="month" SIZE=3 MULTIPLE>. Press [Enter]. Type: <OPTION SELECTED VALUE="april">April. Press [Enter]. Type: <OPTION VALUE="may">May. Press [Enter]. Type: <OPTION VALUE="june">June. Press [Enter]. Type: <OPTION VALUE="july">July. Press [Enter]. Type: <OPTION VALUE="august">August. Press [Enter]. Type: <OPTION VALUE="september">September. Press [Enter]. Type: <OPTION VALUE="october">October. Press [Enter]. Type: </SELECT>. ◥ The Multiple attribute (at the end of the Select Name opening tag) allows form users to select more than one option within the scroll box. A Selected attribute designates the list menu or scroll box option that you want to be selected by default. A Checked attribute designates a default selection in a set of option buttons or check boxes.

6. Click File. Click Save. Your document should look like Figure 4-7.

7. Save the file as form.html. If you open the form page in your browser, it should look like Figure 4-8. Close the browser.

more

The attributes added to the Select tag make it a scroll box or list menu. If you specify a size that size specifies the number of options to be displayed, the options are listed in a scroll box. If no size is given, then the options are displayed in a list menu. You may also add the Multiple attributes. This attribute allows the user to select multiple options, and is displayed as a scroll box.

The value attached to each selection will be used later when the form is submitted. These values will be used to collect information.

Figure 4-7 A list menu and scroll box in an HTML document

Option tag indicates the options to be listed in the list menu

Size indicates how many options are displayed

Figure 4-8 List menu and scroll box in a browser

Click arrow, then click option to make a selection in the list box menu

Three options displayed in the scroll box

Practice

Create a list menu on the pracform page. The text should read: How many times have you been to an accountant?. The options are, 0, 1–3, 4–8, 9–12, 13 or more. Specify the default selection.

skill | Adding Command Buttons to a Form

concept

Command buttons are used to perform preset functions on a form. The most common command buttons are the Submit and Reset buttons. If you want the information completed in the form delivered to another computer that will receive and process the information in some way, you must create a Submit button. Reset buttons allow the user to clear the form of any information entered in the current session. The Submit and Reset buttons usually appear at the bottom of the form, but they can be placed anywhere that is convenient.

do it !

Add two command buttons to the form page.

1. Open the form document in Notepad. Place the insertion point after the last closing </SELECT> tag. Press [Enter] twice.

2. Type: <P><INPUT TYPE="SUBMIT" VALUE="Send Order">.

3. Press [Enter].

4. Type: <INPUT TYPE="RESET" VALUE="Reset Form"></P>.

5. Click File. Click Save. Your document should look like Figure 4-9.

6. Save the file as form.html. Open the form page in your browser. It should look like Figure 4-10.

more

If you want a Submit or Reset button with an image, you will have to use the Button tag. For example, <BUTTON TYPE="submit" NAME="submit" VALUE="submit"><IMG SRC="compass.gif">Send Order</BUTTON>. Using the Button tags (as opposed to the Input Type tags), the value attribute does not designate the text that will appear on the button. The button text is entered before the closing button tag. The button tag is a new HTML 4 feature. You can also change the font, font size, and background color of a button with the Button tag. Use the Style attribute to designate the changes. For example, STYLE= font: 24 pt Arial Black; background:cyan.

If you do not enter a value attribute for the Input Type tag, the default Submit message is Submit Query. The default Reset message is Reset.

Figure 4-9 Command buttons in an HTML document

Tags for the Submit and Reset buttons

Value is the button label

Figure 4-10 Command buttons displayed in a browser

Buttons will appear pressed if you click them

Practice

Add a Submit and Reset button to the bottom of the pracform page. The text on both buttons should simply be Submit and Reset.

Using HTML

skill | Sending Information from a Form

concept

As we said earlier, processing forms is a complex procedure, beyond the scope of this book. This exercise describes a method for sending unprocessed forms, one at a time, directly to an e-mail address. It will familiarize you with the HTML tags and attributes for submitting forms. Generally, the Form tag will include the URL of the CGI script, not an e-mail address. The Submit button will send the data to the CGI script on the server to process your forms. The CGI script will take the name-value pairs (visitor_name=smith) from all the forms, parse and collate the data, and send a report back to your Web site.

do it !

Collect the information from the form page that is sent to an e-mail address you specified.

1. Open the form document in Notepad. Place the insertion point inside the opening Form tag, before the second angle bracket, >.

2. Press the Space Bar.

3. Type: METHOD="POST" ACTION="mailto:orders@officeunbound.domain.com".

4. Click File. Click Save. Your document should look like Figure 4-11.

5. Save the file as form.html. View the form in your Web browser, then close the form document in Notepad.

more

If someone entered data in the current finished form on a Web browser, then clicked the Send Order button, the data would go nowhere because the e-mail address in the mailto section of the form.html file is fictional. However, if the e-mail address was valid, clicking the button would send the form data to that address, usually via the default e-mail program on the source computer. At the e-mail destination, a CGI-script (often linked to a database application) would receive and process the data. For example, the script might return a confirmation message to the sender, prepare a report of names and answers to questions, or so on. Someone at the e-mail destination also could display the data in any number of programs. For example, displaying the raw data in a Web browser could look like Figure 4-12.

There are two methods for sending information to the CGI script on the server: POST and GET. The POST method sends a file with the name-value pairs, the content type, and content length to the server where the CGI script analyzes the data. The GET method adds the name-value pairs to the end of the URL and passes the information on through another set of variables that must be broken down by the CGI script before they can be analyzed. In layman's terms, the results of the two methods differ in that the GET method may result in data being abridged. For this reason, most people recommend the POST method.

There are many ready-to-use CGI scripts to be found on the Web. You will simply have to download one, open it up, and change the pathnames and variables to suit your needs. Most servers require that all CGI scripts be located in a cgi-bin directory. Form hosting services will provide you with a form template to revise and edit as necessary.

Figure 4-11 Specifying how information is to be collected

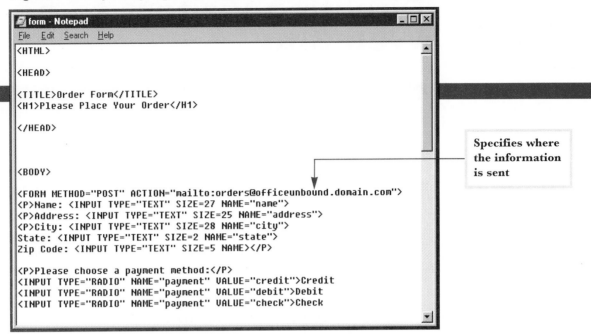

Specifies where the information is sent

Figure 4-12 Information from a form sent via e-mail

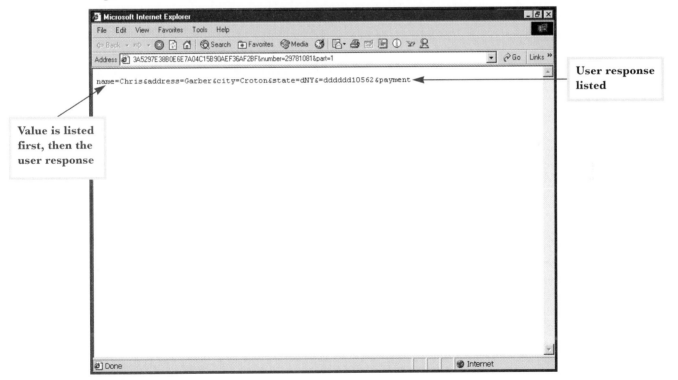

User response listed

Value is listed first, then the user response

Practice

Send the information from the pracform page to the e-mail address, DKnobly@personalaccount.domain.com.

skill | Directing Visitors to a Web Site

concept

As the Web expands, it becomes increasingly unlikely that Web surfers will accidentally hit upon your page. Most people use search engines to locate pages dealing with specific subjects. Users enter keywords to "tell" the search engine what they are looking for. You can use the META tag to designate keywords and describe your Web site for search engines.

do it !

Use the Meta tag so users searching for pages with similar topics will find the Office Unbound Web site.

1. Open the home.html in Notepad.

2. Place the insertion point after the <HEAD> tag.

3. Press [Enter].

4. Type: <META NAME="keywords" CONTENT="Office Unbound, management training, retreats, vacations, teamwork, survival techniques">.

5. Press [Enter].

6. Type: <META NAME="descriptions" CONTENT="a new experience in management training, for learning teamwork">.

7. Press [Enter].

8. Type: <META NAME="author" CONTENT="Tom Randes">.

9. Click File. Click Save. Your document should look like Figure 4-13.

10. Close the file.

more

You should carefully choose the words you use to describe your Web site. For example, the word management is too broad. More specific terms should weed out people who are not interested in management training retreats.

Many search engines provide tips on how to use the Meta tag effectively. If you have a favorite search engine, visit its Web site and read its tips to ensure that your Web page will be found through its searching methods.

Figure 4-14 shows the page source for the United States Department of Labor home page. It displays the keywords, and the description used by their Web designer to describe the Web site. These keywords and description will help lead Internet users to this site, if they are looking for a related topic. It is a good idea to add misspelled words to your keywords. Sometimes users misspell words, and this will help them find your Web site anyway.

Figure 4-13 Meta tags in HTML

For searches that use keywords

For searches that use descriptions

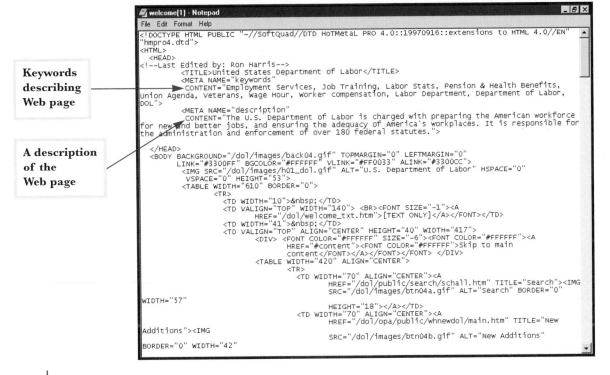

```
home - Notepad
File  Edit  Search  Help

<HTML>

<HEAD>
<META NAME="keywords" CONTENT="Office Unbound, management training,
retreats, vacations, teamwork, survival techniques">
<META NAME="description" CONTENT="a new experience in management
training, for learning teamwork">
<META NAME="author" CONTENT="Tom Randes">
<IMG SRC="compass.gif">
<TITLE>Office Unbound-A New Direction in Management Training</title>
<H1>Office Unbound&#174;</H1>
</HEAD>

<BODY>
<I>A survival retreat, where your management personnel can get to know
one another, enjoy a natural setting together, and most importantly,
learn to work together, as a team.</I>

<PRE>Call
        <U>1-800-555-4563</U>
                   to make an appointment today.</Pre>

<P>"Our management crew was disorganized, and ineffective, but after
the Office Unbound experience they're functioning as one big team."</P>
<BR>Nancy Villones</BR>
```

Figure 4-14 Page Source for Department of Labor Home page

Keywords describing Web page

A description of the Web page

```
welcome[1] - Notepad
File  Edit  Format  Help
<!DOCTYPE HTML PUBLIC "-//SoftQuad//DTD HoTMetaL PRO 4.0::19970916::extensions to HTML 4.0//EN"
"hmpro4.dtd">
<HTML>
  <HEAD>
<!--Last Edited by: Ron Harris-->
    <TITLE>United States Department of Labor</TITLE>
    <META NAME="keywords"
    CONTENT="Employment Services, Job Training, Labor Stats, Pension & Health Benefits,
Union Agenda, Veterans, Wage Hour, Worker compensation, Labor Department, Department of Labor,
DOL">
    <META NAME="description"
    CONTENT="The U.S. Department of Labor is charged with preparing the American workforce
for new and better jobs, and ensuring the adequacy of America's workplaces. It is responsible for
the administration and enforcement of over 180 federal statutes.">

  </HEAD>
<BODY BACKGROUND="/dol/images/back04.gif" TOPMARGIN="0" LEFTMARGIN="0"
    LINK="#3300FF" BGCOLOR="#FFFFFF" VLINK="#FF0033" ALINK="#3300CC">
    <IMG SRC="/dol/images/h01_dol.gif" ALT="U.S. Department of Labor" HSPACE="0"
    VSPACE="0" HEIGHT="53">
    <TABLE WIDTH="610" BORDER="0">
        <TR>
            <TD WIDTH="10"> </TD>
            <TD VALIGN="TOP" WIDTH="140"> <BR><FONT SIZE="-1"><A
                HREF="/dol/welcome_txt.htm">[TEXT ONLY]</A></FONT></TD>
            <TD WIDTH="41"> </TD>
            <TD VALIGN="TOP" ALIGN="CENTER" HEIGHT="40" WIDTH="417">
                <DIV> <FONT COLOR="#FFFFFF" SIZE="-6"><FONT COLOR="#FFFFFF"><A
                    HREF="#content"><FONT COLOR="#FFFFFF">Skip to main
                    content</FONT></A></FONT></FONT> </DIV>
                <TABLE WIDTH="420" ALIGN="CENTER">
                    <TR>
                        <TD WIDTH="70" ALIGN="CENTER"><A
                        HREF="/dol/public/search/schall.htm" TITLE="Search"><IMG
                        SRC="/dol/images/btn04a.gif" ALT="Search" BORDER="0"
WIDTH="57"
                        HEIGHT="18"></A></TD>
                        <TD WIDTH="70" ALIGN="CENTER"><A
                        HREF="/dol/opa/public/whnewdol/main.htm" TITLE="New
Additions"><IMG
                        SRC="/dol/images/btn04b.gif" ALT="New Additions"
BORDER="0" WIDTH="42"
```

Practice

Add keywords and a description to the pracform page. Also specify yourself as the author of this page. Make sure the keywords and description that you provide are appropriately descriptive.

skill | Publishing Web Pages

concept

After you have added all of your objects, elements, and hyperlinks, formatted your text, added color, and refined your page layout to create an attractively spaced document, it is time to publish your site.

The first step is to organize your files. Create one folder for all your files. Place your HTML source documents in the folder. You can either put all your images in the same folder or create an images subfolder. These organizational tasks can be completed as you are creating your site, but you may find it easier to organize everything at the end.

There are several programs you can use to publish your Web site to an Internet Service Provider (ISP). You can use Fetch for Macintosh or WS_FTP for Windows. Both of these programs will walk you through the process of uploading files.

Before you upload your Web pages you will need to contact the server to find out what their protocol is. They may want you to set a password to ensure that you are the only one who can upload files to a particular location. You will also need to get the URL from your ISP and find out what name they want you to assign to your home page. After you have this information, you can use an FTP program such as Fetch, or WS_FTP to transfer your files to the server.

If you used relative URLs, they will not change when you upload your files. As long as they are all in the same folder, the pathnames will not have to be adjusted. If you used absolute URLs, on the other hand, you will either have to change them to reflect the file's new location, or change them to relative URLs.

Figure 4-15 displays the NOAA home page, while Figure 4-16 shows you the HTML source of the NOAA home page, as it is displayed in a browser. Both of these pages feature many of the Web page elements that you have learned about in this book.

Figure 4-15 NOAA home page displayed in a browser

Image added
to a Web page

Hyperlinks in
a Web page

Figure 4-16 HTML source of NOAA home page

A table in
HTML

A table row
in HTML

shortcuts

Form Elements	Opening Tag	Closing Tag
The contained elements are part of a form	<FORM>	</FORM>
Create a text box	<INPUT TYPE="TEXT">	
Create a large text box	<TEXTAREA>	</TEXTAREA>
Create an option button	<INPUT TYPE="RADIO">	
Create a check box	<INPUT TYPE="CHECKBOX">	
Create a list menu	<SELECT>	</SELECT>
Create a scroll box with 'n' number options	<SELECT SIZE=N>	</SELECT>
Set default option	<OPTION SELECTED>	
Insert a submit button	<INPUT TYPE="SUBMIT">	
Insert a reset button	<INPUT TYPE="RESET">	

A. Identify Key Features

Name the items indicated by callouts in Figure 4-17.

Figure 4-17 A form in an HTML document

B. Select the Best Answer

10. Input fields on a form are also known as

11. Text entry fields are also known as

12. Use this attribute to mark the default option in a list menu

13. Without this button information cannot be collected from a form

14. The two methods for submitting a form are Post and

15. This tag adds elements to a Web page that are not visible when a page is displayed

16. To publish your Web pages you must submit them through

17. Rather than displaying text, a password box usually displays

a. Asterisks

b. Controls

c. Get

d. ISP

e. Meta

f. Selected

g. Submit

h. Text boxes

quiz (continued)

C. Complete the Statement

18. Tools that allow users to enter information onto a form are called:

a. Boxes

b. Form tools

c. Input fields

d. Entry parameters

19. The size value of a text entry field is measured in:

a. Pixels

b. Characters

c. Inches

d. Centimeters

20. Option buttons and check boxes which have the same value for this attribute are considered a group:

a. NAME

b. SIZE

c. OUTPUT

d. VALUE

21. The size value for a scroll box designates:

a. How many options you can select

b. How many options are available

c. How many options have the same value

d. How many options are displayed on the Web page

22. Use this attribute to specify keywords or write a description of the Web page:

a. TYPE

b. ATTRIBUTE

c. VALUE

d. CONTENT

23. A more complicated way of collecting information from a form is using this type of script:

a. Common Gateway Interface

b. Common Form Interface

c. Form Interface Script

d. Script Gateway Form

24. To create a password text box, use this tag:

a. <INPUT TYPE="PASSWORD">

b. <PASSWORD SIZE=n>

c. <PASSWORD NAME>

d. <INPUT="PASSWORD">

25. When publishing a Web page, you generally must:

a. Contact an Internet Service Provider (ISP) to find out what their Web protocol is.

b. Set a password to ensure that only you can upload files to your Web site.>

c. Get a URL and Home Page name from the ISP.

d. All of the above.

interactivity

Build Your Skills

1. Add a text entry field to a form:

   a. Create a new text document in Notepad.

   b. Create the basic HTML page structure.

   c. In the Body section of the document create a form.

   d. Within the form, create two small text boxes, for first name and last name, and one large text box for address.

   e. Save the document as orders.html.

2. Add option buttons and check boxes to a form:

   a. Add a group of three option buttons and one check box to the orders form.

   b. The text to accompany the option buttons is: How will you be paying for this order? The option button options are Credit, Debit, Check.

   c. The text for the check box is: Click here if this is a new account.

   d. Save the document as orders.html.

3. Create a list menu on the orders form:

   a. The text accompanying the menu is: Select the style you would like to purchase.

   b. The style options are: Alligator, Renegade, Maverick, Tidal, Coastal, Sonic, and Aero. The default selection is Tidal.

   c. Save the document as orders.html.

4. Collect information from a form:

   a. Add two command buttons, one submit button and one reset button to the bottom of the orders form.

   b. Add a Method attribute and an Action attribute to the Form tag so that the information submitted is by Post, and sent to the e-mail address, info@sunglasscity.domain.com.

5. Help visitors find a page.

   a. Add a Meta tag with these keywords to the Head section of the orders form: orders, shopping, sunglasses, secure shopping, online shopping.

   b. Add this description and another Meta tag to the orders form: An online shopping experience designed to bring the latest fashions in sunglasses to you, the consumer.

   c. Save the document as orders.html.

interactivity (continued)

Problem Solving Exercises

1. Great Work! You only have one more page to create for the Fixit Company, a form. First, create the HTML document in Notepad. Begin with the basic structure for every Web page. Then add the necessary input fields to enable efficient information gathering for the Fixit Company. They want the last name, first name, and middle initial for every visitor. Include controls for collecting the address, including an apartment # field. Next, collect credit card information, including expiration date. (Remember, some of these input fields may not vary greatly. Option buttons or drop-down menus may facilitate data entry.) The company wants to identify its customers as private consumers, construction companies or hardware stores. It also wants to determine if they are first time customers, and if not, what method they used to buy products in the past. For example, were their purchases via the Internet, mail order, or from one of their stores. Choose appropriate controls and save the document as hardware.html.

2. Add some more controls to the hardware form you have been working on. Begin by creating a list menu. The Fixit Company wants the menu to display options about the delivery process. Type: Choose a delivery option. The delivery options are: Next day, Two days, within 5 days, within a week, or by special appointment. Once you have finished this menu you must create a scroll box. The scroll box will display who is going to pay the bill, i.e., who is being charged for the supplies. The options are: your company, the person who is having it delivered, a third party, or a third party company. Once you have finished creating the scroll box, add two command buttons to the form. Add one submit button and one reset button. Make sure that the Form tag is written so that information from the form will be sent to the e-mail address info@fixit.domain.com. Save the document as hardware.html.

3. Create a new document and save as fixit4.txt. Create a link from the fixit page to the hardware page. Create three Meta tags. The first Meta tag should list the keywords: hardware, construction, supplies, personal tools, appliances, online supplies, online shopping, and secure shopping. Next, add a Meta tag with the company description: The Fixit Company, an online hardware store providing products to construction companies, hardware suppliers, and the private consumer. Finally, create a Meta tag that provides the author's name. Your name will be listed as the author's name. Save the document as fixit4.html.

4. Open the personal3.html file from Lesson 3 and save it as personal4.html. Create a new page called guest. Make it a guest book where visitors can sign in. You can create several controls to elicit feedback from visitors. For example, you can collect their names, addresses, and telephone numbers, to compile a mailing list. If you are going to advertise your page, compiling the demographics of your visitors is a good idea. Find out their age, sex, and geographical area. Select appropriate controls and create Submit and Reset buttons. Construct the Form tag so that the information is submitted to your e-mail address. Create a hyperlink labeled Home, to connect the guest page to the personal4 page. Create another hyperlink labeled Guest book, to connect the personal page to the guest page. Format the guest page to complement the style and tone you set for the Web site. Save the file as guest.html, and test the Web site in several browsers. Verify that all the hyperlinks are working and that your information is consistently presented. Complete any final formatting changes. If you already have an ISP, you are ready to follow their instructions and publish the site.

appendix

A. Tag and Attribute Reference Guide

<Tag>/Attribute	Function
<A>	**Creates an anchor or link**
ACCESSKEY	Creates a keyboard shortcut to the link
HREF	Specifies the URL of the target
NAME	Marks an area on a page to jump to
<AREA>	**Specifies coordinates of an image map**
ACCESSKEY	Creates a keyboard shortcut to a hotspot
COORDS	Specifies the coordinates for a hotspot
HREF	Specifies the URL target of the hotspot
NOHREF	Creates hotspots with no target
SHAPE	Specifies the shape of the hotspot
<B>	**Displays text in boldface**
<BGSOUND>	**Adds background sound to a page**
LOOP	Specifies how many times the sound should play
SRC	Specifies the location of the sound
<BIG>	**Makes text appear bigger**
<BLINK>	**Makes text disappear and reappear**
<BLOCKQUOTE>	**Contained text is blocked off separately from rest of text**
<BODY>	**Contained text makes up the Body section of the page**
ALINK	Specifies the color of an active link
LINK	Specifies the color of a new link
VLINK	Specifies the color of a visited link
BACKGROUND	Adds a background image to a page
BGCOLOR	Adds a background color to a page
TEXT	Specifies the color of text for the page
** **	**Creates a line break**
CLEAR	Stops a text wrap around the sides of an image
<BUTTON>	**Creates a button**
ACCESSKEY	Creates a keyboard shortcut for the button
NAME	Identifies the button
TYPE	Specifies the type of button to create
<CAPTION>	**Creates a caption for a table**
ALIGN	Aligns the caption above or below a table
<CENTER>	**Used to center text, images, and other objects**
<CITE>	**Contained text is a citation or quotation**
<CODE>	**Contained text is a computer code**
<DD>	**A definition in a list**

A. Tag and Attribute Reference Guide (continued)

<Tag>/Attribute	Function
<DL>	**Creates a definition list**
<DT>	**Contained text is a definition term**
<EM>	**Emphasizes text**
<EMBED>	**Embeds multimedia files in a page**
ALIGN	Aligns controls
AUTOSTART	Starts multimedia file automatically
CONTROLS	Displays play, pause, and rewind buttons
LOOP	Specifies how many times multimedia file should play
SRC	Specifies the location of the multimedia file
<FONT>	**Formats text on a Web page**
COLOR	Specifies text color
FACE	Specifies text font
SIZE	Specifies text size
<FORM>	**Creates a form**
ACTION	Specifies where the information from a form will be sent
METHOD	Specifies the method of collecting information from a form
<Hn>	**Creates a Header (n=number of header)**
ALIGN	Aligns the Header
<HEAD>	**Contained text is part of the Head section of the page**
<HTML>	**Contained text is written in HTML**
<I>	**Italicizes text**
<IMG>	**Inserts an image**
ALIGN	Aligns the image
ALT	Displays text if image is unavailable
BORDER	Adds a border to an image
CONTROLS	Adds video controls to a multimedia file
LOOP	Specifies how many times a video should run
SRC	Specifies the location of an image
START	Specifies when a video should start
USEMAP	Specifies what image map is being used

A. Tag and Attribute Reference Guide (continued)

<Tag>/Attribute	Function
<INPUT>	**Creates an entry field or control on a form**
ACCESSKEY	Creates a keyboard shortcut to a form object
CHECKED	Makes a radio button or check box selected by default
DISABLED	Disables a form object
MAXLENGTH	Specifies maximum characters allowed to be entered
NAME	Identifies the data collected by a form
SIZE	Specifies the size of text boxes
SRC	Specifies the location of an image
TYPE	Determines type of entry field or control to be added
VALUE	Specifies value of options on a form
<KBD>	**Specifies keyboard text**
<LI>	**Contained text is a list item**
TYPE	Specifies the symbols used to mark each list item
VALUE	Specifies value of a list item
<MAP>	**Creates an image map**
NAME	Names an image map so it can be referred to later
<MARQUEE>	**Creates moving text**
BEHAVIOR	Specifies how the text moves, slides, scrolls, alternates
DIRECTION	Specifies the direction in which the text moves
LOOP	Specifies how many times the text repeats
<META>	**Specifies information about a Web page**
NAME	Specifies the type of information being described
CONTENT	Describes the Web page
<OL>	**Creates an ordered list**
TYPE	Specifies symbols to mark each list item
START	Specifies value for each list item
<OPTION>	**Creates a group of options in a form**
SELECTED	Specifies the default option
VALUE	Specifies values of menu options
<P>	**Creates a new paragraph**
ALIGN	Aligns the paragraph
<PRE>	**Displays text exactly as it appears in HTML document**
<Q>	**Contained text is quoted**
<S>	**Displays text with a line through it, same as <STRIKE>**
<SAMP>	**Displays text in a monospaced font**

A. Tag and Attribute Reference Guide (continued)

<Tag>/Attribute	Function
<SELECT>	**Creates a menu in a form**
NAME	Identifies data collected in form
MULTIPLE	Allows the user to select multiple options
SIZE	Specifies the size of the menu, visible on the screen
<SMALL>	**Makes text appear smaller**
<STRIKE>	**Displays text with a line through it, same as <S>**
<STRONG>	**Emphasizes text**
<SUB>	**Displays text as subscript**
<SUP>	**Displays text as superscript**
<TABLE>	**Creates a table**
BGCOLOR	Specifies the background color of a table
BORDER	Specifies the thickness of the border
BORDERCOLOR	Specifies the color of the border
CELLPADDING	Specifies the amount of space between a cell's contents and border
CELLSPACING	Specifies the amount of space between cells
<TD>	**Creates a table cell**
ALIGN	Aligns contents within a cell
BGCOLOR	Specifies the background color of a cell
ROWSPAN	Specifies how many rows a cell should use
<TEXTAREA>	**Creates a large text box**
ACCESSKEY	Creates a keyboard shortcut to the text box
NAME	Identifies the data collected from the form
ROWS	Specifies the number of rows in the text box
COLS	Specifies the number of columns in the text box
<TH>	**Creates a Header in a table**
ALIGN	Aligns the Header in a cell
BGCOLOR	Specifies the background color in the Header's cell
ROWSPAN	Specifies how many rows the Header should use
<TITLE>	**Creates the title in the Title bar area**
<TR>	**Creates a row in a table**
ALIGN	Aligns the data in a row
BGCOLOR	Specifies the background color for a row
<TT>	**Displays monospaced font**
<U>	**Underlines contained text**
<UL>	**Creates an unordered list**
<VAR>	**Displays variable text**

B. Special Character Codes

Character	Code	Character	Code
Å	Å or Å	Õ	Õ or Õ
Æ	Æ or Æ	Ö	Ö or Ö
à	à or à	Ø	Ø or Ø
á	á or á	Œ	Œ or Œ
â	â or â	ò	ò or ò
ã	ã or ã	ó	ó or ó
ä	ä or ä	ô	ô or ô
å	å or å	õ	õ or õ
æ	æ or æ	ö	ö or &ouml
È	È or È	ø	ø or &oslash
É	É or É	œ	œ or œ
Ê	Ê or Ê	Ù	Ù or Ù
Ë	Ë or Ë	Ú	Ú or Ú
è	è or è	Û	Û or Û
é	é or é	Ü	Ü or Ü
ê	ê or ê	ù	ù or ù
ë	ë or ë	ú	ú or ú
Ì	Ì or Ì	û	û or û
Í	Í or Í	ü	ü or ü
Î	Î or Î	Ÿ	Ÿ or Ÿ
Ï	Ï or Ï	ÿ	ÿ or &yuml
ì	ì or ì	Ç	Ç or Ç
í	í or í	ç	ç or ç
î	î or î	ß	ß or ß
ï	ï or ï	Ñ	Ñ or Ñ
Ò	Ò or Ò	ñ	ñ or ñ
Ó	Ó or Ó	!	&#33;
Ô	Ô or Ô	"	" or "

B. Special Character Codes (continued)

Character	Code	Character	Code
#	&#35;	¶	¶ or ¶
$	&#36;	·	· or ·
%	&#37;	ª	ª or ª
&	&#38 or &;	º	º or º
*	&#42;	»	» or »
@	&#64;	¼	¼ or ¼
~	~ or ˜	½	½ or ½
ƒ	ƒ or ƒ	¾	¾ or ¾
…	… or …	¿	¿ or ¿
†	† or †	∂	ð or ð
‡	‡ or ‡	<	< or <
‰	‰ or ‰	>	> or >
•	• or •		
™	™ or ™		
¡	¡ or ¡		
¢	¢ or ¢		
£	£ or £		
¥	¥ or ¥		
§	§ or §		
¨	¨ or ¨		
©	© or ©		
«	« or «		
®	® or ®		
°	° or °		
±	± or ±		
`	&#96;		
´	´ or &acute		
µ	µ or µ		

C. Guide to the Sixteen Predefined Colors

Color Name	Color
Black	
Silver	
Gray	
Purple	
Navy	
Blue	
Cyan	
Maroon	
Red	
Magenta	
Olive	
Green	
Lime	
Teal	
Yellow	
White	

D. Guide to Hexadecimal Color Values

Hexadecimal Code	Color
#7FFFD4	
#8A2BE2	
#5F9EA0	
#008B8B	
#483D8B	
#00BFFF	
#00CED1	
#1E90FF	
#ADD8E6	
#B0C4DE	
#E0FFFF	
#66CDAA	
#0000CD	
#191970	
#B0E0E6	
#87CEEB	

D. Guide to Hexadecimal Color Values (continued)

Color Name	Color
#7FFF00	
#006400	
#556B2F	
#8FBC8F	
#228B22	
#ADFF2F	
#7CFC00	
#90EE90	
#32CD32	
#3CB371	
#00FA9A	
#F5FFFA	
#98FB98	
#2E8B57	
#00FF7F	

D. Guide to Hexadecimal Color Values (continued)

Hexadecimal Code	Color
#FF7F50	
#DC1436	
#8B008B	
#8B0000	
#E9967A	
#FF1493	
#B22222	
#FF69B4	
#CD5C5C	
#FFB6C1	
#FFA07A	
#FFE4E1	
#FFA500	
#BC8F8F	
#FA8072	

D. Guide to Hexadecimal Color Values (continued)

Color Name	Color
#FFF8DC	
#B8860B	
#FFD700	
#DAA520	
#F0E68C	
#FFFACD	
#EEE8AA	
#FFEFD5	
#D2B48C	
#F4A460	
#8B4513	
#BDB76B	
#D2691E	
#DEB887	
#A52A2A	

D. Guide to Hexadecimal Color Values (continued)

Color Name	Color
#9400D3	
#E6E6FA	
#FFF0F5	
#9370DB	
#C71585	
#DA70D6	
#DB7093	
#DDA0DD	
#EE82EE	
#BA55D3	
#9932CC	
#640537	
#ED9DCA	
#FD00CB	

D. Guide to Hexadecimal Color Values (continued)

Color Name	Color
#FAEBD7	
#F0FFFF	
#F5F5DC	
#FFE4C4	
#FFEBCD	
#FFFAF0	
#DCDCDC	
#F8F8FF	
#FFFFF0	
#FAF0E6	
#FFE4B5	
#FFDEAD	
#FDF5E6	
#FFDAB9	
#FFF5EE	
#F5F5F5	

D. Guide to Hexadecimal Color Values (continued)

Color Name	Color
#F5DEB3	
#FFFAFA	
#708090	
#778899	
#DCDCDC	
#696969	
#2F4F4F	
#A9A9A9	
#A1A1A1	
#404040	
#212121	

glossary

Absolute pathname

A method of naming the location of objects and images, by describing the direct path to get there, including listing all of the folders that need to be opened.

Action

An attribute that tells a browser where to send the information from a form; it can be mailed to an e-mail address or sent to a Web page, which has a CGI script.

Adobe PageMill

An HTML editor that allows you to create Web pages graphically while the program writes the HTML for you.

Adobe Photoshop

An image editing program which can be used to find the RGB content of colors, used for Hexadecimal values, or used to locate pixel coordinates to create an image map.

Align

An attribute that moves any object, including text, to the left , right, or center of a page.

Anchors

A way of marking objects or text so that a link may be created that connects a user to the location of the anchor.

Angle brackets (< and >)

These are symbols created by using your keyboard; all tags, attributes, and values are written within angle brackets.

Area tag

A tag that allows you to specify the pixel coordinates of an image map, or hot spot.

Attributes

Used with tags and values, attributes are used to describe the way an object should be displayed by a browser.

Background color

The color that appears on the background of a Web page, specified by the hexadecimal values of colors.

Background sound

Sound that can be added to a Web page, so that the sound will be heard whenever the page is opened.

Backspace key

A key on keyboards that allows users to delete text that appears on the page in Notepad.

Big

A physical character tag that makes text appear larger.

Body

A tag that specifies to browsers that the contained text is part of the Web page; this section makes up most of the Web page.

Bold

A physical character tag that instructs a browser to display text in bold.

Border

Lines that can be added to, and surround images and tables; the thickness and color of borders may be specified with certain attributes.

Browser

See Web Browser.

Bulleted list

A list that does not have a specific order, so the list items are marked with bullets rather than numbers or letters. This is the same as an Unordered list.

Cell

The empty spaces that are created by the rows and columns of a table. Contains the information in a table.

Character tag

A type of tag that tells a browser to display text a certain way; there are two types of character tags: physical and logical.

Check box

A check box is another way of answering a yes or no question. The user has an option of checking the box to select it (a yes answer) or not checking it (a no answer). Check boxes may also be used in place of radio buttons.

Circle

A value used with the Shape attribute to specify the shape of a hotspot on an image map, specified in x, y, r coordinates.

Clear

An attribute used with the line break tag that stops a text wrap at a specified location.

Click

To press and release a mouse button in one motion; usually refers to the left mouse button.

Code

A logical character tag that tells a browser to display the text in a fixed-width font.

Column

A vertical grouping of cells in a table, often containing related types of text and/or data.

Common Gateway Interface (CGI)

A programming language used to create scripts that are used to extract information collected from a form.

Coordinates

Used to specify the exact location of a hotspot on an image map, by using the x, y location of pixels on an image.

Control

An object that makes data entry easier and more efficient; most controls appear on form pages, such as check boxes, and radio buttons.

Desktop

The standard Microsoft Windows screen; it is designed to have the appearance of an actual desktop.

Definition list

A list that includes a description for each term; the type of list one might find in a dictionary or glossary of terms.

Dialog Box

A box that groups functions together; it performs certain actions depending on the commands you use and the options you select.

Drop-Down Menu

See pull-down menu.

EM tag

A logical character tag that instructs a browser to emphasize the contained text, usually emphasized in bold.

E-mail link

A hyperlink that opens a browser's mail program with an e-mail address specified so the user can send e-mail to the specified location.

Embed tag

A tag used to embed multimedia files on a Web page, it works with a Netscape plug-in that allows users to control the way multimedia files are displayed.

f

Fetch

A program for Macintosh computers that moves files from your computer to a location provided by an ISP.

File

A menu on the Menu bar; it provides commands that have to do with saving, opening, printing, storing, and performing other filing options on your HTML pages.

Font

The style in which text appears. Bold, italic, script, serif, and sans serif are all styles associated with different fonts.

Font tag

The tag that makes formatting changes to text, you can use this tag to affect size, color, and other formatting options.

Form page

A type of Web page that asks the user for information; once the information has been entered, the page may be sent to the Web manager and saved to a page with a CGI script, or sent to an e-mail address so the data can be recorded.

Form tag

The tag that specifies that the contained text is to be included with the form, and how the data will be collected when the form is submitted.

Formatting

The process of adding elements to your Web page, including objects, text, colors, and other important Web components to give your pages a certain look or style, and make it attractive.

Graphics

Another term used to describe images that appear on a Web page.

Graphic Interchange Format (GIF)

A format in which images are saved, where the image is compressed so that it does not take up much space, and doesn't take long to download.

Head

A tag that specifies that all contained text will appear in the head section of the Web page.

Headers

Tags used to format text so that they will appear in one of six Header formats used to mark sections on a Web page.

Hexadecimal color values

A way of coding colors so that they can be specified on a Web page. The format is #RRGGBB, and based on the RGB, or Red Green and Blue content of the color.

Home page

The first page that a visitor sees when they enter your Web site. It is where they begin to navigate through the site.

Hotspot

The area on an image map formatted so that the area is linked to a target page. When clicked, the hotspot acts as a hyperlink.

HREF

The attribute that specifies the URL of the target page that the hyperlink will link to. The URL can be relative or absolute.

Hyperlink

A hyperlink is a piece of text that links to another Web page.

Hypertext Markup Language (HTML)

The standardized computer language used for defining the way information and/or graphics appear on a Web page.

I-beam

When you move the mouse pointer over text or an area of a page where text may be inserted it turns into an I-beam; so named because it looks like an I-beam.

Icon

A small graphic that identifies an object.

Image Edit

An image editing program that may be used to identify the pixel coordinates of an image so that they may be used to create an image map.

Image map

An image that is formatted so that a particular spot on the image is linked to a target page. When clicked the spot acts as a hyperlink.

Image tag

The tag that is used to format and insert an image; there is no closing tag required for this tag.

Inline image

An image that appears with a Web page when it is opened in a browser; it does not have to be downloaded.

Input field

Another name for a control on a form. Input fields are used to collect data from a user in the form of text boxes, radio buttons, check boxes, etc.

Input tag

The tag that adds an input field to a form; used with the Type attribute, it specifies the type of input field that will be added to a form.

Insertion point

A flashing point on a page, it marks the point where text will be entered on the page.

Internet

A global network of computers exchanging information over the network, it includes the Web servers, the individual user, and organizations that manage the networks.

Internet Explorer

A Web browser create by Microsoft; it is the most popular browser used to search the Internet.

Internet Service Provider (ISP)

An Internet service provider is simply a company that manages locations and files on the Internet, so that you can publish pages, and search the Internet.

Italics

A physical character tag that tells a browser to display the contained text in italics.

Joint Photographic Experts Group (JPEG)

A format in which images are saved, where the image is compressed so that it does not take up much space, and doesn't take long to download.

Keyboard shortcut

A way of interacting with objects on a Web page using the keyboard with shortcuts that were programmed into a Web page.

Keywords

The attribute used with the Meta tag used to describe a Web page so that visitors will be able to find your page.

Line break

A tag used to create spacing in a Web page; the spacing between line breaks is less than with paragraphs.

List

A list is a way of organizing information on a Web page by displaying it in list format.

List item

A tag that allows you to add more items to a list.

Logical character tag

A character tag that tells a browser to perform a certain function on text; it does not specify exactly how the browser should perform this action.

Macromedia Dreamweaver

An HTML editor that allows you to create Web pages graphically while the program writes the HTML for you.

Map tag

The tag that is used to create an image map; it specifies the image to use, which is referenced using the Usemap attribute.

Menu

A list of related commands.

Menu bar

Found below the Title bar, it contains the names of menus that present lists of commands to choose from.

Meta tag

A tag used to describe your Web pages so that search engines and users searching the Internet will be able to locate your Web page.

Method

An attribute that describes the way data will be collected from a form; the two methods are Post and Get.

Microsoft FrontPage

A graphical HTML editor that adds objects to Web pages for you, and writes the HTML code.

Mouse pointer

The arrow-shaped cursor on the screen that you control by guiding the mouse on your desk. The shape of the mouse pointer can change depending on the task being executed.

Multimedia file

Files that are added to a Web page that do more than still images and graphics. Sound, video, and animation are examples of multimedia files.

Nested list

A list in which each list item contains another list within it; the second list is nested within the first.

Netscape Navigator

A Web browser created by Netscape; it is a popular browser used to search the Internet.

Notepad

A text editor program found on Windows; used to write and edit text, it may be used to create HTML documents.

Numbered list

A list whose list items are arranged in a specific order so they are marked by numbers or letters; this is the same as an Ordered list.

Option button

A small circular button, generally in a dialog box or a form, that anables you to select one choice from a set of choices; also called a radio button.

Option tag

A tag used to create an group of options on a form in the format of a pull-down menu.

Ordered list

A type of list in which the the list items are ordered by marking them with numbers, letters, or roman numerals.

Page Setup

A dialog box that allows you to set printing options for printing documents; it is accessible from the File menu.

Paint Shop Pro

An image editing program that allows you to locate pixel coordinates on an image in order to specify the coordinates on an image map.

Paragraph tag

A tag that creates spaces on a Web page; these spaces are greater than the spaces created by line breaks.

Password

An input type that creates a password text box that displays asterisks or bullets rather than the text the user is typing.

Pathname

A way of specifying the locations of pages and objects. There are two ways of specifying pathnames, relative and absolute.

Physical character tag

A character tag that instructs a browser exactly how to display the text.

Pico

A text editor program for Unix systems that allows you to write and edit text, and create HTML documents.

Pixels

Locations on an image, specified in x, y coordinates that are used to specify the location and size of hotspots on image maps.

Polygon

A value which specifies that shape of a hotspot on an image map, it is specified in x, y, x1, y1, x2, y2 coordinates.

Preformatted text

Text that is contained within tags that instruct the browser to display it exactly as it appears in the HTML document.

Print

A command found on the File menu that allows you to print a copy of the Notepad screen, so that you can have a hard copy of the document you are working on.

Properties

A button available on the Print dialog box that allows you to select the print options available.

Pull-down menu

Controls that are added to a form; they display only one option, but if you click a down arrow a menu appears with more options.

Push button

A button that is added to a form page that allows a user to submit a form or to reset a form; these options may be set when the button is created.

r

Radio button

See "Option button."

Rectangle

A value that is used with the Shape attribute to specify the shape of a hotspot on an image map; specified with x, y, x1, y1 coordinates.

Relative pathname

A pathname that specifies the name of a file but not the exact location. This is useful if all of the files are located in the same folder.

Reset button

A push button added to a form that allows the user to reset the form, and clear all the information from the input fields.

Row

A horizontal grouping of cells within a table, often containing data related to one record.

Save

A command found on the File menu that saves a file simply by overwriting the existing saved document.

Save As

A command found on the File menu that allows you to save a file with a new name and a new location.

Scroll box

A control added to a form that displays several options at once, and allows the user to scroll through the menu of available options.

Size

An attribute used with several different tags that allows the user to specify the size of objects and text.

Small tag

A physical character tag that tells a browser to display the text in a smaller font.

Source

An attribute that uses pathnames to specify the location of an image or a multimedia file so it can be displayed on a Web page.

Special characters

Characters and symbols that do not appear on a keyboard that can be inserted onto a Web page by using special codes.

Strong tag

A logical character tag that tells a browser to emphasize the contained text.

Submit button

A push button added to a form that allows the user to send the data filled out on a form to the specified location.

Table

An object that you can insert into a Web page to help organize information. The table is made up of rows and columns which create cells, the cells contain the information.

Table header

A tag that allows you to add a cell with a Header; these Headers are useful for organizing information in a table.

Table row

A tag that creates a new row of cells in a table; you can add as many rows as necessary to a table.

Tags

Commands written in HTML that instruct a browser how to display objects and text that are specified, and contained within the tags.

Target

The page, or location that a hyperlink links to. When creating a hyperlink the target page or URL must be specified. The target page must also be in working order for the hyperlink to work.

TeachText

A text editor program that allows you to write and edit text, and is used to create HTML documents.

Text box

See Text entry field.

Text editor

A simple word processing program that allows you to write and edit text, and allows you to create HTML documents.

Text entry field

Controls that are added to a form that allow the user to enter data into a text box, whose size is specified.

Title

A tag that creates a title for your page, this title will appear in the title bar of a browser whenever your Web page is opened.

Title bar

The bar that appears at the top of the browser window; it displays the title of the page that is specified in the HTML document that is being displayed.

Underline

A physical character tag that instructs the browser to display the contained text underlined.

Uniform Resource Location (URL)

The address of a Web page. Every page has its own URL; no two URLs are exactly the same.

Unordered list

A list that does not have a specific order, so the list items are marked by bullets rather than numbers or letters.

Usemap

An attribute that allows you to specify the image you would like to use to create an image map from; the image map is referenced with the Map tag.

Values

Specify how an attribute will affect the Web page by specifying how the browser should display it.

Web Browser

A program that has the ability to display Web pages, and can access them off of the Internet, it displays pages by reading the code they are written in.

Web Page

A document that appears on the Internet with its own URL. It may contain graphics, text, or any number of elements that may be viewed once it is published.

Web Server

A computer running software that stores Web pages and objects, so that when a browser requests a page or object, the server furnishes the request. The browser interprets the objects as pages, text, graphics, etc.

Web site

One or more Web pages that are linked and may be navigated by a visitor. Web sites are managed and owned by a person, company, or an organization.

Windows Taskbar

Usually located at the bottom of your desktop screen, it contains buttons that allow you to open programs and perform certain functions.

Wordpad

A text editor program that allows you to write and edit text, and allows you to create HTML documents.

Wrapping text

A method of designing Web pages so that when an image inserted, the text is displayed next to the image for as far down as the image goes on the page.

WS_FTP

A program used with Windows that moves your files from a computer to an ISP so you can publish and update Web pages.

index

The table below summarizes the external data files that have been provided for the student. Many of the exercises in this book cannot be completed without these files. The files are distributed as part of the Instructor's Resource Kit and are also available for download at http://www.mhhe.com/it/cit/index.mhtml. Please note that the table below only lists the raw files that are provided, not the versions students are instructed to save after making changes to the raw files or new files that the students create themselves.

Lesson	Skill Name/Page #	File Name	Introduced In
Lesson 1	Opening a Document to View its HTML Structure/HT 1.8	htdoit1-4.txt	do it! step 4
	Opening a Document to View its HTML Structure/HT 1.9	htprac1-4.txt	Practice
	Writing Tags and Editing HTML Pages/HT 1.13	htprac1-6.txt	Practice
	Saving Pages/HT 1.14	htdoit1-7.txt	do it! step 2
	Saving Pages/HT 1.15	htprac1-7.txt	Practice
	Interactivity	htskills1.txt	Build Your Skills #2c
Lesson 2	Using Titles/HT 2.2	home.txt	do it! step 1
	Creating Lists/HT 2.10	htdoit2-5.txt	do it! step 1
	Understanding Anchors/HT 2.14	htdoit2-7.txt	do it! step 1
Lesson 3	Inserting Images/HT 3.4	htdoit3-2.txt	do it! step 1
	Inserting Images/HT 3.4	Unbound.jpg	do it! step 4
	Inserting Images/HT 3.5	htprac2.jpg	Practice
	Adding Multimedia Files/HT 3.12	home.txt	do it! step 1
	Adding Multimedia Files/HT 3.12	compass.gif	do it! step 4
	Adding Multimedia Files/HT 3.13	Sound3.wav	Practice
	Interactivity/HT 3.25	htskills3-1.jpg	Build Your Skills #1b
Lesson 4	Adding Text Entry Fields/HT 4.4	htdoit4-2.txt	do it! step 1
	Directing Visitors to a Web Site/HT 4.14	home.html	do it! step 1